The Upside Down Way

The Upside Down Way

Following Jesus through the Gospel of Luke

Matthew Ingalls

WIPF & STOCK · Eugene, Oregon

THE UPSIDE DOWN WAY
Following Jesus Through the Gospel of Luke

Copyright © 2017 Matthew Ingalls. All rights reserved. Except for brief quotations in critical publications or reviews, no part of this book may be reproduced in any manner without prior written permission from the publisher. Write: Permissions, Wipf and Stock Publishers, 199 W. 8th Ave., Suite 3, Eugene, OR 97401.

Wipf & Stock
An Imprint of Wipf and Stock Publishers
199 W. 8th Ave., Suite 3
Eugene, OR 97401

www.wipfandstock.com

PAPERBACK ISBN: 978-1-5326-0536-9
HARDCOVER ISBN: 978-1-5326-0538-3
EBOOK ISBN: 978-1-5326-0537-6

Manufactured in the U.S.A.   JANUARY 18, 2017

Scripture quotations marked (NRSV) are taken from the *New Revised Standard Version Bible*, copyright 1989, Division of Christian Education of the National Council of the Churches of Christ in the United States of America. Used by permission. All rights reserved.

Scripture quotations marked (NIV) are taken from the Holy Bible, *New International Version*®, NIV®. Copyright © 1973, 1978, 1984, 2011 by Biblica, Inc.™ Used by permission of Zondervan. All rights reserved worldwide. www.zondervan.com The "NIV" and "New International Version" are trademarks registered in the United States Patent and Trademark Office by Biblica, Inc.™

For my boys
The Way is not of will, but grace

Contents

Acknowledgments | ix
Introduction | xi

1 Questions Are the Beginning of Discipleship | 1
2 Learning to Run Again | 5
3 All the Baptists and Republicans with Me! | 10
4 That Hairy Lunatic in the River | 13
5 Jesus ≠ Power | 17
6 From Marveling to Maleficence | 20
7 Anger in Politics | 24
8 The Credibility of Humility | 28
9 Scarred by Affection | 32
10 Which Jesus? | 35
11 Where Is Your Faith? | 39
12 Fear in the Way | 41
13 Breaking Down the Kitchen Door | 45
14 Money, Health, and Striving | 48
15 Marching up the Hill | 53
16 Swallow Jesus? | 57
17 Yours or Ours? | 61

Contents

18 Include Lazarus | 65
19 It Matters Where We Begin | 69
20 The Poor Investor | 72
21 All of Patrick | 76
22 Our Last Table | 80
23 The God Who Suffers and Is with Us | 84
24 An Upside-Down Sentence | 88
25 Suffering, Even on Sunday | 91

Bibliography | 95

Acknowledgments

To look to Jesus is to look to the community that he has gathered and is gathering around him. The writing journey that follows in these pages is the overflow of my interaction with this big and very old community. I owe thanks to men and women long passed, like Felicitas, John Chrysostom, and Patrick of Ireland. I am also indebted to the kind-hearted contributions of Jesus' current followers. River Street Church of God, the congregation I pastor, has spent the last six years encouraging me and fostering me in a way that made this book possible. My friend Gwendolyn Leininger offered this work both her impeccable editor's eye and her bursting theologian/poet heart. Debbie read my first thoughts and coaxed me into believing I had the start of a real book. Arthur spoke light when my spirit went dark. And Ben sacrificed much of his sabbatical to read this and give me another pastor's perspective. I even stand on the shoulders of my high school English teachers. I would not have known I could write if Mrs. Mullet and Mrs. Helfrich had not told me so.

I did not launch into this adventure the moment it popped into my head and heart. No, I let it sit there for

ACKNOWLEDGMENTS

years, too afraid to make the leap between dream and reality. But as always, it was my wife and her unflinching "go for it," that gave me the courage to put the lessons of my soul into these devotionals. Her partnership finds itself quietly dispersed among these pages in ways too sacred to make explicit. I have these words to say, because of who I have become walking next to her.

And finally, I must thank my parents, who tolerated my incessant questions and never squelched my desire to both understand and imagine. There were many times that the institutional structures of the church threatened the flourishing of my mind, but my parents always insisted on letting me come to Jesus on my own terms. It is to their credit that I have fixed my gaze on Jesus and his way.

Introduction

And Mary said,

> My soul magnifies the Lord, and my spirit rejoices in God my Savior, for he has looked with favor on the lowliness of his servant.
>
> He has shown strength with his arm; he has scattered the proud in the thoughts of their hearts.
>
> He has brought down the powerful from their thrones, and lifted up the lowly; he has filled the hungry with good things, and sent the rich away empty.
>
> LUKE 1:46–53 (NRSV)

MARY WAS NO QUEEN. She did not rule anyone. There was no throne in her home; no noble privilege, no power for hire, or riches for use. Every other woman from this period who shared her socio-economic status—poor, single, and uneducated—is lost to obscurity. If you were a first-century Jew looking for hope in your world of oppression, you would not have knocked on Mary's door. You would have ignored her in all your plots and dreams for liberation from

Introduction

the heavy hand of Rome and its surrogates. If it had been up to you, hope for humanity would never have come from the untouched womb of a simple young woman.

Make no mistake, the Jews of Mary's age *were* looking for hope. The Romans occupied the land of Israel, stabilizing it with brutality toward dissenters. The temple and the religious system that revolved around it were corrupted by greed and pagan Roman influence. These Jews lived daily in fear of death. They needed some hope. And lots of people offered it, perhaps none more so than Herod the Great.[1] He had hoped that the Jews would embrace him as their savior—he had, after all, built a world-famous temple for the people and their God. This temple was gigantic, inlaid with gold, visible for miles . . . a truly exceptional mark of God's glory in the landscape of Israel. The Jews believed that this holy temple was the only place on earth where humans could offer sacrifices to God. They thought that God's heavenly throne literally penetrated our world within the Holy of Holies. Even if Herod was awful, the temple was where God lived. And truly, Herod was awful. His throne was tainted with innocent blood and overshadowed by Roman influence. Religiously devout Jews heartily ignored him as savior and, for their own safety, tolerated him as king. At the same time, they did indeed put their hope in the grand temple he built.[2]

Meanwhile, in little ol' Bethlehem, through lowly and inconsequential-to-history Mary, God was being born. While the people were looking to the glorious, erudite,

---

1. There were many factions vying for the attention of hopeful Jews: Sadducees, Herodians, Zealots, Pharisees, and the Essenes. For a further explanation of these groups see chapters 2 and 3.

2. There were a few Jewish groups who weren't sold on the temple, like the Qumran community who kept and compiled the famous Dead Sea Scrolls.

Introduction

and powerful trappings of their religious system God was descending into their world in the humblest of fashions. It's upside-down. We want God to be golden, shiny, and illustrious. He's small, a baby, dirty, crying, and wrapped in strips of cloth. We want to know where he'll be; say, in the temple or church. And when he'll be there; like the Day of Atonement and Passover or Sunday morning. Instead, he shows up in the middle of the night, noticed only by some unassuming shepherds.

Again, so upside-down.

But if you think the beginning is upside-down, just wait for the end. Victory through death? That's crazy.

The book of Luke, in particular, is the story of Jesus living a very upside-down life. It is also the story of Jesus inviting people into his upside-down way of life. And not just upside-down for the sake of being upside-down. No, upside-down because the traditional methods for connecting with God were flawed. If you want to get to know God, begin with humility. Start with compassion. Get going with generosity. Want to save your life? Lose it. Want to love God? Love people. Want to see holiness? Look at broken people.

I haven't written anything new so far. The life of Jesus has been meticulously documented, but the implementation of that study leaves something lacking. We have books about Jesus that capture the church's imagination, but barely skirt the actual text of the Gospels. Then we have research works so thick with technical language most people only pretend to understand them.[3] I long for a treatment of Jesus' life that takes the text of scripture seriously and con-

---

3. The disunity between the world of the church and the academic study of Jesus bothers and baffles me. Who could benefit more from a serious and thorough look at Jesus? I hope to pack complex historical and theological ideas into creative and conversational language that directly connects to the reality of the church.

nects to our imaginations regarding how we might actually live and worship.[4] And so, on the one hand, I write in order to meet that need.

On the other hand, I write because the upside-down way of Jesus changed my life. I write because I believe the church needs this way. Even more, the world needs a church that walks the upside-down road. I write because I think the world and God's church will flourish with the flourishing of Jesus and his lifestyle.

I grew up with Jesus. I asked him to rule my life when I was three. I was on my dad's shoulders, on a walk looking at snow-covered nativities, when I said, "Jesus, please live in my heart!" It's a kitschy story, but looking back I feel like I was a boy asking a wild lion to lead me. I had no idea what Jesus would teach me and ask of me. That he'd whisper in my soul, "Love your enemy," and actually mean it. That he'd teach me the deepest theology through the poorest and most uneducated of people. That he'd make me laugh on street corners with drug addicts. That he'd teach me to devalue shiny Christianity and to cherish the faith of those struggling to get by. That he'd walk me into the insidious self-despair of perfect strangers. That he'd lead me into the darkest corners of my own soul. Or that he'd teach me the joy of a life lived upside-down.

And so I humbly offer the following devotions drawn from Jesus' life according to Luke. For years, I've suggested that searching people read Luke in one sitting. Each Gospel has its own strengths. For Luke, it's Jesus' upside-down way of life. No other Gospel takes such pains to highlight Jesus' bizarreness. You don't need historical study to get that from Luke, but I think if you consider Jesus' historical reality and his social world you really begin to realize that he was

4. There are other works that accomplish this, though they are few. For an example, see Wright, *Luke*.

INTRODUCTION

beautifully irrational. So, I've done my best to include good historical research in my interpretations and applications. You can look to my footnotes for sources, corresponding scriptures, and snarky comments.

If nothing else, I hope you'll learn to forget the kings and temples or the glitz and glamor. I hope that you'll learn to see that the path to overcoming leads not through great halls, high arches, or holy rooms, but in humble moments of self-sacrificing love. I hope you learn to disdain Herod's greatness and, instead, go looking for hope amongst lowly servants. I hope that you'll learn something about following Jesus in his ridiculous plot to undo sin and redeem his creation. I hope it makes your head spin. I hope you feel a little topsy-turvy. I hope you begin to feel like up is down and down is up. Kings are peasants and peasants are queens. Temples are empty and empty-spaces are temples. Like Jesus has turned your life upside-down.

Matthew Ingalls
Newberg, Oregon
May, 2016

1

Questions Are the Beginning of Discipleship

Zechariah asked the angel, "How can I be sure of this? I am an old man and my wife is well along in years." The angel said to him, "I am Gabriel. I stand in the presence of God, and I have been sent to speak to you and to tell you this good news. And now you will be silent and not able to speak until the day this happens, because you did not believe my words, which will come true at their appointed time."

LUKE 1:18-20 (NIV)

DO FAITH AND QUESTIONS go together? Normally if we say that someone is "questioning their faith," we don't mean something good is happening. And this story of Zechariah seems to only support that perspective—he asks a question only to have his vocal chords decommissioned.

But I think the reason questions have not found a happy home in the pews has little to do with Zechariah. Instead, it seems to me that we're scared of questions. We often seem to think that questions and atheism go hand-in-hand. Those who deny the existence of God are normally there because they couldn't get past a big question. A question like, *how could a good God let the world be so bad?* Or they have questions about the Bible, science, miracles, etc. We see their questions and associate them with their atheism/agnosticism. That, in turn, makes us scared that if we let the people we love ponder the big questions they might go down the road toward disbelief.

Another reason I think we have a history of antagonism toward questions has to do with the way we've been instructed to read scripture. When I was a kid I remember being taught that Jonah's problem was that he questioned God.[1] I also remember being taught that James 1:6–8 was about people filled with questions:

> But when you ask, you must believe and not doubt, because the one who doubts is like a wave of the sea, blown and tossed by the wind. That person should not expect to receive anything from the Lord. Such a person is double-minded and unstable in all they do (NIV).

Is it possible that "the one" filled with doubts is someone the writer actually knows rather than a dictum meant to describe every doubt from then until eternity? Jesus, for one, showed great compassion to at least one man struggling with doubts (Mark 9:24).

It was also drilled into me that the Bible was without error and therefore must never be questioned. The ironic thing is that the Bible is the very reason I now value questions. The Bible is full of people asking sincere questions. Consider Psalm 94:3, "How long, LORD, will the wicked,

---

1. Jonah's problem was his prejudice against the Ninevites. See Jonah 4:2 and chapter 12 of this book.

Questions Are the Beginning of Discipleship

how long will the wicked be jubilant?"[2] We must acknowledge that the writer's question itself is not atheistic. In fact, this is one of the most important questions for us to ask. It illustrates our deep desire for justice and equality in the world. It comes from our cross-refined compassion for those trampled under injustice. It is among the holiest of questions. The Psalms, prophets, and Lamentations are full of people asking God questions. God did not terminate them. So too, in the first chapter of Luke, right alongside Zechariah, another person is asking a question:

> "How will this be," Mary asked the angel, "since I am a virgin?" (v. 34, NIV).

An innocent, young girl asks God, via Gabriel, a very sincere question. And she gets a very straightforward and sincere answer. No fire from the sky. No "tisk, tisk." No "how dare you ask a question!"

So what makes Mary and Zechariah different? For one, Mary is asking the question, "how?" *How* is an awesome question! *How* is innocent. *How* flows from wonder and interest. Zechariah, on the other hand, has an angel standing before him and asks for a sign. It's like I give you a piece of cake and you say, "will you bring me some dessert?" If you said, "how'd you make this awesome cake?" you'd be paying me a compliment. You'd be interested in my process, my creation, my plan. Zechariah's question diminishes what God has done by sending him an angel and asks for God to do even more.

I pray that I would be a pastor and author full of questions. I pray that I would be like Mary, marveling at the goodness of God's work and entering into His action with sincere questions. I've written this study of Luke to give you

---

2. See also, Hab 1 for an authentic exploration of this question before God.

a chance to ask Jesus and his church your questions. I want the church to be a place where questions do not paralyze us, but a place where questions are a part of our activity. A place where a little girl can ask, "how," and get a compassionate and straightforward response. My point is when we ask Jesus questions he leads us into great places. Not comfortable places, as we'll see, but life-changing places.

Before I end, one more thought: Gabriel was straightforward with Mary, but in no way did he *solve* all the questions. The virgin birth is a mystery. No one can ever fully explain how she birthed God's Son. You can keep asking how, and eventually, no matter who you're asking, they're going to have to say, "I don't know." That doesn't mean we ask a bunch of questions and come up empty handed. Instead, as we inquire and journey onward we find that our questions, by grace, have brought us quite close to the unfathomable God.

2

Learning to Run Again

Then his father Zechariah was filled with the Holy Spirit and spoke this prophecy:

> Blessed be the Lord God of Israel, for he has looked favorably on his people and redeemed them. He has raised up a mighty savior for us in the house of his servant David, as he spoke through the mouth of his holy prophets from of old, that we would be saved from our enemies and from the hand of all who hate us. Thus he has shown the mercy promised to our ancestors, and has remembered his holy covenant, the oath that he swore to our ancestor Abraham, to grant us that we, being rescued from the hands of our enemies, might serve him without fear, in holiness and righteousness before him all our days.
>
> LUKE 1:67–75 (NRSV)

My Misery

For me, 2013 was a very difficult year. Among the reasons, I spent the first six months unable to run. I normally run every day for forty-five minutes to an hour. To me, running is sacred space. It has always been a place where God seems close; where my mind's air is clearer, ideas brighter, and stress smaller. In January of 2013 I hurt my knee. I tried all sorts of healing and recovery methods, but nothing worked. I was miserable. I felt crushed under the weight of this injury; spoiled by my helplessness. I was frustrated because I couldn't do something I felt created for; separated from my sacred space.

The injury made me rather gruff and wearisome to be around. There was something about this frustration, this debilitating weight that made me feel like I couldn't be myself. It was as if the effervescence of my soul had gone flat. Perhaps you too have some space in your life that is sacred. What would it do to you to have that suddenly taken away? Some calling? Some purpose? Some activity? Gone.

Israel's Injury

> Now the Lord said to Abram, "Go from your country and your kindred and your father's house to the land that I will show you. I will make of you a great nation, and I will bless you, and make your name great, so that you will be a blessing. I will bless those who bless you, and the one who curses you I will curse; and in you all the families of the earth shall be blessed" (Gen. 12:1–3, NRSV).

When the people of Israel thought about their calling they thought about Abraham (Abram above). God spread open a sacred calling for Abraham and his children, a path for them to dutifully tread. And the entire human race stood to benefit from their running that path well. But in the days of Jesus, Israel was wounded and incapable of rising to run the race for which they were created. They were not the people God designed them to be. For a variety of reasons, stringing back to Abraham himself, they were a people crushed under the weight of their mistakes, their idolatry, their xenophobia, and the oppression of history's largest militaries (Assyria, Babylon, Persia, Greece, and finally Rome). The combination of these forces kept them from living out Abraham's calling—to be harbingers of God's love for the whole world.

At the time of Zechariah's song a man named Herod the Great sat on the "throne." But he was a "vassal king," meaning he served the interest and authority of Rome. Herod built a temple in Jerusalem.[1] At the gate of the temple Herod built a gold statue of an eagle. The eagle was a symbol for Rome. So at the entryway of God's holy house stood the emblem of Antiquity's great and bloody empire. Jews hated that eagle. It represented Rome's paganism, violence, and taxes. It also represented Herod's unequal and burdensome taxes that bankrolled the temple project. It was a symbol for the centuries Israel had spent injured, unable to run where God had called them.

And they were frustrated by their injury. They were all hoping and wanting to undo the wounds and regain some ability to be Israel. That's really all the Pharisees were. They were people who really wanted to heal their people. They just wanted to do it by following the law exactly as they interpreted it. Zealots were motivated by the same desire. But they wanted to do it by violently overthrowing the powers of Herod and Rome and to then create an Israel completely free of foreigners. You can imagine the angst, bitterness,

---

1. This is the same temple Jesus critiques, questions, and clears.

and frustration that pervaded every Jewish home. One day, around the time of Jesus' birth, some young Jewish radicals destroyed Herod's eagle.[2] Herod, being the gracious even-tempered guy that he was, executed them. Shortly thereafter Herod died. For a small period after Herod's death Judaea had no king/ruler. The leadership vacuum created a giant revolt, every group vied for control. The revolt was crushed, the land divided between three of Herod's sons, real authority was vested in Roman procurators (i.e. Pontius Pilate), and Israel was right back where she had been for centuries: injured, wounded, and powerless.

Jesus was born before Herod's death. So he had to have been born in 4 B.C. or just a touch earlier.[3] Which means that Zechariah's song above, reflects feelings from the last years of Herod's bloody and oppressive reign. His joy, and Mary's in verses 46–55, come from wounded hearts, battered by the daunting weight of a people's sin, unfair kings, and tyrannical empires. They cried out in joy because finally their nation had a chance to move on from their injuries and run into their divine destiny: to bring reconciliation between God and creation.[4]

The healing, the recovery, the hope comes in a Bethlehem manger. While the whole Jewish world is either scrounging for power through persuasion and violence or wallowing in the pain of their wounds, God was moving in a teenage girl. God was speaking to Zechariah. God was to be born in their midst, almost unnoticed. God was coming

---

2. Josephus, *War*, 1:33:1–3.

3. The reason Jesus wasn't actually born in the year 1 A.D. is because of a miscalculation on the part of a medieval monk named Dionysius.

4. If you think I should have written, ". . . between God and humans," read Rom 8:18–25 and Col 1:15–20. These passages suggest that the benefits of Jesus' work will rescue all of creation from the curse of sin.

naked, vulnerable, and crying—just like us. Their wounds so great from time and bitterness that God came humbly to be with them; be with us. And Jesus does show them and us a way to live free from the oppressive weight, free to be the proclaimers of God's full love for his creation. As Zechariah realized, he would pick them up and graciously show them (us) how to run again.

3

All the Baptists and Republicans with Me!

"When the angels had left them and gone into heaven, the shepherds said to one another, 'Let us go now to Bethlehem and see this thing that has taken place, which the Lord has made known to us.' So they went with haste and found Mary and Joseph, and the child lying in the manger. When they saw this, they made known what had been told them about this child; and all who heard it were amazed at what the shepherds told them."

LUKE 2:15-18 (NRSV)

IN THE PREVIOUS DEVOTION I wrote about the different factions in ancient Israel—Pharisees and Zealots. It is important to know that there were a lot of different groups vying for power and influence in Palestine. Along with the Pharisees and Zealots there were Sadducees, Essenes, the mysterious community at Qumran, and just normal people trying to live out their faith and lives.[1] These groups all had

1. For more on these groups see respective articles in Green,

positions: pro-temple, anti-temple; pro-Rome, anti-Rome; violence, pacifism; resurrection, no resurrection; waiting for a priestly messiah, warrior messiah, or many messiahs. They disagreed about how to relate to non-Jews. They had arguments about what could be learned from Greek philosophy. They even divided over how to interpret the Bible.

When Jesus comes, his first cries break forth into a divided and disorderly world. These shepherds (and the Magi in Matthew) hear that a king has been born in Bethlehem, hurry to see him, and Joseph stops them at the cave entrance and says, "Are you a Torah-believing Pharisee?"[2] Uh, what?

No, no, no! What matters is how they respond to the king in the manger as he is, not as they expect him. Consider the experience of Simeon:[3]

> It had been revealed to him by the Holy Spirit that he would not see death before he had seen the Lord's Messiah. Guided by the Spirit, Simeon came into the temple; and when the parents brought in the child Jesus, to do for him what was customary under the law, Simeon took him in his arms and praised God . . . (Luke 2:26–28, NRSV).

Simeon was awaiting this child; this boy; this king; this God. And when he saw him he says, "Thank God! Now everyone will know that the Essenes were right!" Huh?

No, Simeon is swept *away from* the divisive allegiances of his age and *into* a connection with Jesus. Simeon's hope is in him, what he will do, and who he will become. He has to leave the factions behind.

McKnight, and Marshall, *Dictionary*.

2. In case the "cave," reference threw you: there's as good a chance that the manger of Jesus' birth was located in a cave rather than a wooden-frame stable.

3. There's also the prophet Anna, whose story is not as detailed, but very similar to Simeon's (Luke 2:36–38).

The Upside Down Way

Is our world so different? I suggest that no allegiance in our lives, no amount of philosophizing, no grand doctrines will ever replace the experience of beholding the King. When he comes again to reclaim what's his I don't think he'll say, "Okay, all the Baptists and Republicans with me. Off with the rest of you." What *will* matter is our relationship with him. Because the end of time won't be about us and how right or wrong we all were. It is all about him. He will set things right. He will do what needs to be done. He will decide what justice and mercy look like. He will be the light at the center of the city.[4] And like the shepherds and Simeon did long ago, we too will watch him with wonderment and praise. And we too will have no hope outside of our trust in him. We will have to accept him as he is, not as we or our party would like him to be. The shepherds paid royal homage to a baby born in a barn, wrapped in tattered cloth, mothered by a virgin. How many of our allegiances might prevent us from taking such a leap faith?

I don't think we have to wait for the end of time to receive our King. As we reflect on the manger let us grab hold of the child who has already come. Let us hold him high in the arms of our hearts and praise God for his presence in our midst. Let us make him the center of who we are. Let us give him the lead. Let us follow him into holiness and love. Let us grow up with him. Let us keep our eyes fixed upon him. Let us refrain from thinking that our allegiance to this world's organizations will matter. Let us crown him King.[5]

---

4. I'm thinking about the images of Rev 21. If you want to think about what will matter at the end of things, that's a pretty good place to look.

5. I am not saying that you can just believe any old thing or that how you live your life doesn't matter. What I am saying is that it all starts not with how we live or what we believe but with our response to Jesus. If we make Jesus our king, our center, our foundation, and our light, it would stand to reason that we would take his teachings on theology and how to live with the utmost seriousness. In fact, I

4

That Hairy Lunatic in the River

It's all gone dark. Your people are oppressed, mostly impoverished, illiterate, many of your babies die within their first two years, forty years is a good long life, crops are hard to come by, and even your most sacred sites languish in the shadows of Rome's harsh standards.¹ It used to be that your people heard from God often. It used to be that your people felt God actively working on your behalf. Now it's just dark.² Your leaders seem to be more concerned with how they appear, their status, and the weight of their purse than with real reform, or real devotion to God. Their holiness, to you, looks a lot more like wealth and oppression than an imitation of the God you grew up worshiping. Your land is not your own, you are not free, your leaders are corrupt, you struggle to get bread, and disease, illness, and the hardness of life constantly threaten the lives of your people.

---

would say that the primary result of making Jesus our king is that he sets about to completely change who we are now and eternally.

1. For an excellent description of the harshness of life in the 1st century see Malina and Rohrbaugh, *Social-Science*, 1–17.

2. The prophets warned Israel about this darkness. See Mic 3:5–12.

The Upside Down Way

All is dark. Will God ever come back and be your king once more?

Enter John, son of Zechariah and Elizabeth. At first he seems a little bit crazy, a hairy lunatic wading in the Jordan. He wears strange things, he lives in the wilderness, and eats bugs. But his message is the first glimmer of real hope in a long time.[3]

What is his message? God is sending someone to inaugurate his Kingdom. Be baptized, repent of the grime of this way of life and be clean . . . be ready to participate in what God is about to do. Leave every allegiance and cling to the movement of God. John the Baptizer is the first preacher of God's Kingdom in the New Testament story.[4]

> He [John] went into all the region around the Jordan, proclaiming a baptism of repentance for the forgiveness of sins (Luke 3:3, NRSV).

John is also the first person we know of who utilized public baptism in Judaism.[5] So John comes preaching something

---

3. Josephus tells a story about Athronges, which is helpful. During Jesus' childhood Athronges led a powerful revolt against the Romans. It took Rome a while to organize a defense, but once they did, they brutally crushed the movement. According to Josephus two thousand rebels were crucified and left to decay throughout the Jerusalem countryside. Jospehus, *Ant.*, 17:10:8–10.

4. For clarity's sake, there are others who foreshadow the kingdom before John: his dad Zechariah, the Archangel Gabriel, Mary, Simeon, and Anna. But John is the first to make a vocation out of proclaiming what God's about to do through Jesus.

5. The history of baptism is a fascinating subject. Jews never used baptism, that we know of, before the birth of Christ. Around that time a group in the desert, the Qumran Community, did begin to practice a very similar baptism, but privately. Other religions also used baptism with various meanings. A very popular, illegal and therefore underground pagan religion at the time baptized new members in the blood of a bull. I suppose none of that changes your life, but doesn't it awake the nerd in you a little?

very new: be baptized, because someone is coming to start God's Kingdom and you need the fresh start of baptism to be ready for it. To get ready for what God is about to do you need to repent and be immersed into what God is doing.[6] On the other hand, John's message is really old: repent and be wrapped into God's coming kingdom (see Isaiah and Amos). But what does repent really mean?

Repentance literally means to make a u-turn. In Greek it means a mental u-turn. In Hebrew it can mean to physically be walking one direction and to then turn around and walk the other direction. If you're going to make a u-turn then you must be headed toward one thing and then need to turn back toward another thing. So what did John's listeners need to make a u-turn from? That, in fact, is exactly what they asked him: "And the crowds asked him, 'What then should we do?'"(Luke 3:10, NRSV).

What was John's answer? Say a certain prayer? Go to the altar? Schedule a meeting with the pastor? Never miss Sunday morning worship? Read a Psalm a day? Ditch Chris Tomlin for the Gaithers? Do a capital campaign to make your church building amazing? Vote the way Christian organizations tell us to? Wear a "Repent or Burn" shirt to every social function this year?

> In reply he said to them, "Whoever has two coats must share with anyone who has none; and whoever has food must do likewise." Even tax collectors came to be baptized, and they asked him, "Teacher, what should we do?" He said to them, "Collect no more than the amount prescribed for you." Soldiers also asked him, "And we, what should we do?" He said to them, "Do not extort money from anyone by threats

---

6. The Greek word *baptizō* literally means to dunk and soak in water.

or false accusation, and be satisfied with your wages" (Luke 3:11–14, NRSV).

I can hear them saying, "Is there any way to undo that whole baptism thing? I think I'd prefer the t-shirt option."

All kidding aside, he attaches their baptism and their participation in the coming Kingdom of God to ethics—how they ought to live their lives. Specifically, if they are to participate in God's unfolding work they must inject their daily lives with abounding generosity. Generosity. They are to make a u-turn away from greed and toward generosity.

Into the darkness of greed, corruption, oppression, death, and illness John thrusts a sliver of light: God is about to move, leave the old way of doing things and be ready for what's coming. How? Let your life, your mind, your heart be saturated, immersed, baptized in the generous heart of God. Let the direction of your life be bent in the direction of God's big and generous spirit.

Perhaps you thought he might tell you to sharpen your sword. Or to run away. Or to elect your faction's candidate. Or to put your leaders on trial. Or to defame Caesar.

No. In the darkness, the light and hope of the kingdom begins with generosity.

5

Jesus ≠ Power

Jesus, full of the Holy Spirit, left the Jordan and was led by the Spirit into the wilderness, where for forty days he was tempted by the devil. He ate nothing during those days, and at the end of them he was hungry.

The devil said to him, "If you are the Son of God, tell this stone to become bread."

Jesus answered, "It is written: 'Man shall not live on bread alone.'"

The devil led him up to a high place and showed him in an instant all the kingdoms of the world. And he said to him, "I will give you all their authority and splendor; it has been given to me, and I can give it to anyone I want to. If you worship me, it will all be yours."

Jesus answered, "It is written: 'Worship the Lord your God and serve him only.'"

The devil led him to Jerusalem and had him stand on the highest point of the temple. "If you are the Son of God," he said, "throw yourself down from here. For it is written:

"'He will command his angels concerning you
to guard you carefully;

> they will lift you up in their hands,
> so that you will not strike your foot against a stone.'"

Jesus answered, "It is said: 'Do not put the Lord your God to the test.'"

When the devil had finished all this tempting, he left him until an opportune time.

LUKE 4:1–13 (NIV)

POWER FEELS LIKE VICTORY. It isn't victory, mind you. Victory is an achievement, while power is a resource that may or may not be used to achieve anything. But because power feels like victory it is the object of our constant lust. My dad taught me the absurdity of this perspective. In my first year of college, his boss offered him a promotion. The promotion entitled my dad to more money and the ability to make executive decisions for his department. The praise and trust of his superiors must have felt like a win. If it did, he never shared those feelings with me. He turned the promotion down. "It would take me away from your events . . . with a great promotion comes greater time constraints," he would tell me. He understood the truth: the power inherent in a new position would actually cost him what he loved; what might feel like winning is actually losing.

When I read the temptation of Christ I always wonder if Satan has any right to the power he waves under Jesus' hunger-wearied nostrils. Or is he simply lying; testing Jesus' resolve to love the unlovable? Satan's temptations in Luke's fourth chapter revolve around power. First, end your suffering by trumping the physical make-up of stone with divine fiat. Jesus chooses to keep his stomach miserable, to continue to suffer. Second, forget establishing the Kingdom of God, I'll give you a grand kingdom if you'll serve me. Jesus chooses to continue to raise his kingdom from the ailments and sins of society's untouchables. Finally, prove your anointed position; prove you have the power of God flowing through your veins. Jesus chooses not to use power to prevent his own death. Imagine how awesome any of these three would have felt! How practical they are! Jesus wants to wrap people into the kingdom, what better way than to be a king or to show them all his chosenness by falling into angel-arms from the temple wall. No. Jesus eschews power for the sake of love.

His path to kingship will not rely on illustrations of might. It will rely on fishermen, prostitutes, and tax collectors. It will ride on a donkey, not a war horse. It will fill the aching bellies of the crowd, but not of the king himself. It will climb up a hill to die for sinners, not to show that God would empty heaven to save the chosen one. It will win through lovingly faithful servitude, the antipathy of power.

I have to ask then, why does the church so swoon over power? We will empty our treasuries to secure the victory of a particular candidate. We will bow to deep pocketed elders for the establishment of bigger buildings and more "relevant" programs. We will throw ourselves from the character of Christ in order to be caught by the flying fads and prejudices of our age. Or will we, like Jesus, faithfully cling to the Father's love rather than power?

After all, perhaps power is a mirage in the wilderness; an empty vision of fulfillment and victory, that in truth, only leads to narcissism and self-protective fear. Is power a fictive oasis?

Maybe, in order to enter the victorious kingdom of Christ one must suffer to allow the desire for power to die, so that the desire to love might flourish.[1]

1. I don't mean "enter the kingdom," in the sense of one's salvation as much as discipleship within the kingdom. Think, "If any want to become my followers, let them deny themselves and take up their cross daily and follow me" (Luke 9:23b, NRSV).

6

From Marveling to Maleficence

He began by saying to them, "Today this scripture is fulfilled in your hearing."

All spoke well of him and were amazed at the gracious words that came from his lips. "Isn't this Joseph's son?" they asked.

LUKE 4:21-22 (NIV)

JESUS COMES HOME TO Nazareth as a celebrity. It's no shock then that the leaders of the synagogue pay him the honor of reading from Isaiah. He chooses a great passage about the effects of God's chosen one on Israel's society. Isaiah is full of such promises: when God sends his anointed hero everything from the grass to the lambs will benefit. This particular passage declares that God's activity will help the least fortunate and the most oft forgotten of Israel's people: the poor, the prisoners, the blind, and the oppressed. When Jesus reads it and then says that such activity is happening

From Marveling to Maleficence

through him people say, *Amen!* Who wouldn't want their society to reap such benefits?

If you watch movies that depict this scene they don't follow Luke at this point.[1] They skip ahead to when the people try to throw Jesus off a cliff (v. 29). They paint the picture that people got ruffled by Jesus proclaiming he would be fulfilling the promise. Their storyboard goes like this:

Jesus reads the scroll.

Jesus says he is the messiah.

People freak out at his blasphemy.

They try to kill him.

Jesus uses his divine powers to escape.

The church has long desired to defend Jesus' divinity and one way we've done so is by suggesting that the Jews thought Jesus' messiahship was akin to blasphemy.[2] Nothing could be further from Luke's depiction. Indeed, Nazareth marveled at the possibility that one of their own, from Joseph's humble workshop, might be chosen to bring God's favor. In amazement they speak well of him.

Nevertheless, the story ends with that same crowd trying to throw him off a cliff. So how do they go from marveling to maleficence? Well, Jesus picks a fight:

> Jesus said to them, "Surely you will quote this proverb to me: 'Physician, heal yourself!' And you will tell me, 'Do here in your hometown what we have heard that you did in Capernaum.' Truly I tell you," he continued, "no prophet is accepted in his hometown. I assure you that there

---

1. *The Jesus Film* is a prime example, even though it takes its dialogue almost verbatim from Luke.

2. For a much better argument for the divinity of Christ see Wright, *The Challenge of Jesus*.

were many widows in Israel in Elijah's time, when the sky was shut for three and a half years and there was a severe famine throughout the land. Yet Elijah was not sent to any of them, but to a widow in Zarephath in the region of Sidon. And there were many in Israel with leprosy in the time of Elisha the prophet, yet not one of them was cleansed—only Naaman the Syrian" (Luke 4:23–27, NIV).

Here's my paraphrase: *All that good stuff Isaiah talks about is not just for Israel. In fact, Israel might just miss out on it. The Kingdom of God is going to widows in Zarephath and lepers in Syria!*[3]

For these good, probably quite sincere Jews, God was their God. The Kingdom of God belonged to them. The Covenant belonged to them. Jesus is saying no more. His ministry will intentionally reach out to non-Jews throughout the region. And that's so preposterous and so awful that his hearers judge him worthy of a mob's execution.

We live in a time when God's association to races and their perspectives is as relevant as ever. Too often we neglect a global perspective of our faith for the sake of a sense that God belongs to our own tribe. We watch the latest crisis mostly concerned about how it will all affect us. During the Arab Spring of 2011, one woman at a prayer meeting told me, "We have to pray about the situation over in the Middle East! That could really affect our economy." As she spoke a dictator beat and shot his own people on television. I wonder if Jesus might have said to her: *you think I'm here to protect your economy, but instead I am with those protesters, lying wounded in the streets for their sake. Do you see me?*

---

3. The book of Isaiah makes this rather clear in several places. For a few examples see Isa 52:10, 56:1–8, 60:3–4, and 66:18–23.

From Marveling to Maleficence

That's what I think we should ask when we see riots, police violence, and violence against police. Do we see Jesus on the side of those we oppose? Do we remember that he is their God too? Yes. Jesus belongs to no tribe, yet every tribe shall benefit from his kingdom.

7

Anger in Politics

One day Jesus was teaching, and Pharisees and teachers of the law were sitting there. They had come from every village of Galilee and from Judea and Jerusalem. And the power of the Lord was with Jesus to heal the sick. Some men came carrying a paralyzed man on a mat and tried to take him into the house to lay him before Jesus. When they could not find a way to do this because of the crowd, they went up on the roof and lowered him on his mat through the tiles into the middle of the crowd, right in front of Jesus.

When Jesus saw their faith, he said, "Friend, your sins are forgiven."

The Pharisees and the teachers of the law began thinking to themselves, "Who is this fellow who speaks blasphemy? Who can forgive sins but God alone?"

Jesus knew what they were thinking and asked, "Why are you thinking these things in your hearts? Which is easier: to say, 'Your sins are forgiven,' or to say, 'Get up and walk'? But I want you to know that the Son of Man has authority on earth to forgive sins." So he said to the paralyzed man, "I tell you, get up, take your mat and go home." Immediately he stood up in front of them, took what he had been lying on and went home praising God. Everyone was amazed and gave praise to God. They were filled with awe and said, "We have seen remarkable things today."

LUKE 5:17–26 (NIV)

Jesus' anger in the Gospels is almost exclusively related to one of two things: first, and most often, one group is attempting to limit another group's ability to have a relationship with God. The religious leaders in the Gospels are often convinced that foreigners, lepers, the lame, the blind, tax collectors, prostitutes, women, children, and the impoverished do not deserve the same access to God that the religiously pure deserve.[1]

Second, we see Jesus' anger appear when people put religious traditions in front of the welfare of hurting people—like when religious leaders think Jesus can't heal a man with a withered hand on the Sabbath (Luke 6:6–11). Jesus' challenge to his dissenters is that surely human suffering trumps regulations for weekly rest.[2]

These two causes of Jesus' annoyance are both at the heart of what Jesus is doing in the story above. The

---

1. They also didn't want these folks to have full access to the society of God's people. They thought people's imperfections meant they should be isolated from both God and God's people.

2. Jesus is also famous for chastising his disciples with the invective: "Where is your faith?" I've often wondered if Jesus' language toward his disciples is marked by sadness rather than anger. On the other hand, there's no doubt that many of his words toward the Pharisees and scribes strike an angry tone. For more on "where is your faith," see chapter 11.

Pharisees can't stand for the man's undeserved healing and they can't accept forgiveness that doesn't come from God through the system established at the temple. Never mind that a man who lives on a mat might have a hard time getting to the temple. Jesus hits their calloused assumptions with a powerful display of rebellion; an intentional effort to expose their hard-heartedness.[3]

Everyone is talking about anger in politics these days. And for good reason, everywhere I turn someone is scoffing over a red or blue candidate. It is clear that anger in politics often leads to disrespect, name-calling, and even the audacity to say that someone is disqualified from saving Christian faith because of party affiliation. I often challenge people to take a higher road in politics, to which they invariably respond: "Well Jesus got mad and said harsh things to people." Yes, he did. But in what kind of situations did he say harsh things? He was not a flippant antagonist. And should we not also limit our acted anger to certain arenas? Lest we do violence to the approachability of God's gospel.

So, that political thing that is driving you nuts, is it actually keeping people from being free to begin or to make progress in a relationship with God?

Additionally, are you mad because the pompous and self-righteous attitudes of religious leaders are keeping God's healing and alleviative power from the people who need it most?

In almost every other topic of disagreement Jesus finds a way to be charitable, respectful, to-the-point, and to love the person he is interacting with. My point here is

---

3. It is an interesting question to ask if Jesus is indeed angry here. Perhaps he answered the Pharisees quite calmly. But you don't have to go far in the book of Luke to find Jesus acting out in anger at the Pharisees. See Luke 11:37–54, where Jesus pronounces judgment on the Pharisees and scribes. Each of his indictments fall along the lines of the two causes of anger listed above.

not to tell you not to be angry about political and social situations. My point is that anger must not morph into name-calling, leaping to assumptions, refusing to listen, and the belittling of your opponents. Love is our weapon of persuasion.[4] Love is the way Jesus won his victory. Love is the only way that truth can be proclaimed. When we lose hold of Jesus' love in political discussions we lose the essence of who we are and we fail to imitate our Lord. We can have a perfect knowledge of economics and taxes, but if we have not love then our knowledge is destitute. We can win election after election, but if we have not love then our victory is sorrowfully lost. We can have the perfect plan for the country's future, but if we have not love then our forethought is nearsighted.

May, in these controversial days, we be permeated with the heart of Christ. Caring for what he cares about and caring in the way he cares. May his charity, his patience, his wisdom, his generosity, his faith, his endurance, his servanthood, and his compassion be windows through which we see our world.

---

4. Consider 2 Tim 2:23–24.

8

The Credibility of Humility

JOHN CHRYSOSTOM, ONE OF Christianity's most prolific preachers, delivered his sermons from the ambo—a reading desk on the floor of the sanctuary. People sojourned from the furthest stretches of the Roman world to behold the Gospel on John's lips. Chrysostom spent the final years of his ministry in one of earth's most beautiful churches—the Hagia Sophia, in modern-day Istanbul. The pulpit rose far above the sanctuary floor as a way of reminding churchgoers of the grandness of the word they'd come to hear. It must have been startling then, to watch the frail Chrysostom shuffle up to the reading desk, barely visible. His decision to preach from a place of humility and his policies of simplicity made him a champion of common people in a city fraught with greedy and oppressive elites.[1]

For me, Chrysostom's example elucidates an excellent point about leadership: quality leadership is the result of

---

1. Chrysostom lived from c. 349 to 407 A.D. Those greedy and oppressive elites had him exiled twice and each time common folks rioted in the streets. For a biography on Chrysostom see Kelly, *Golden Mouth*. For a simpler introduction to him, see Chrysostom, *Living*.

authentic credibility. Full-bodied credibility is the result of humility.

Allow me to explain: no one is perfect, right? So if leaders display a life absent of struggle or weakness they are being disingenuous, thus destroying credibility. Therefore, humility is at the heart of establishing credibility. That's why I find it terribly hard to follow most of today's well-known Christian leaders. Many seem to enjoy the lofty location of their pulpits; secure in the distance it creates between their closeted frailty and their target audiences. For a long while, there has been a plague of weakness-denial in American leadership—the Church included. Weaknesses and mistakes are covered up at all cost. We've created a mythic veneer that is destined to fade. Eventually we find out that our leaders are broken; they have addictions; they have a secret lover; they have a mysterious bank account. I'm not saying any of these things are acceptable. However, perhaps they wouldn't have turned to these dark places if, to begin with, there hadn't been the unrealistic pressure of lofty perfection.

Millennials, my generation, are hyper-sensitive to this. Experts say we crave authenticity.[2] We crave an atmosphere where leaders are humble. We yearn for a community of equals who are transparently struggling to follow Jesus. And since we can't seem to find leaders behaving and speaking authentically (humbly) we are deserting the Christian institution.[3] Credibility lost.

> He came down with them and stood on a level
> place, with a great crowd of his disciples and a

---

2. Google, "Millennials value authenticity," and see how many of the links take you to people trying to figure out how to market to my peer group.

3. For an excellent study of the Millennial exodus see Kinnaman and Hawkins, *You Lost Me*.

> great multitude of people from all Judea, Jerusalem, and the coast of Tyre and Sidon. They had come to hear him and to be healed of their diseases; and those who were troubled with unclean spirits were cured. And all in the crowd were trying to touch him, for power came out from him and healed all of them. Then he looked up at his disciples and said . . . (Luke 6:17–20a (NRSV).

In the passage, the bold words of our Lord are not bolstered by arrogance, but by humility's cornerstones: compassion, servanthood, listening, and empathy.[4] In this passage he picks a level place from which to teach and has to look up at his disciples while he talks—therefore, he's either short or sitting. So many of our leaders keep talking down at us and certainly down their noses when addressing the broader populace. How is it that he who had no reason for humility embodied it, while those who have every reason for humility discard it?

So where are the leaders who would speak softly up at the world? Where are our leaders who are washing the feet of their enemies? Where are our leaders who see the potential of the broken? Who decline the favor of fame and influence? Who will serve without prejudice? Who would choose the ambo over the pulpit?

I encourage you to infuse your influence with the credibility of humility. Choose to lead by listening. The influence at the ambo may be limited compared with the wide reach of lofty pulpits, but those who have had the greatest impact on my life bear a greater resemblance to John Chrysostom than to any Christian blogger of today's lot. The humble leaders I know personally don't get much press.

---

4. At first glance you might miss Jesus' listening posture, but if he is healing folks then he is probably giving them space to ask for healing and to explain their ailment.

The Credibility of Humility

They don't speak at large rallies. Most of them don't blog or post on Facebook. No, they're too busy living on a level plane with the broken to get attention from our perfection-driven world. They're too busy leading humbly.

9

Scarred by Affection

"But I say to you that listen, Love your enemies, do good to those who hate you, bless those who curse you, pray for those who abuse you."

LUKE 6:27-28 (NRSV)

My son beat me up over the weekend. My nose and cheeks are full of scratches. He's only seven months old, so he's just beginning to figure out affection. Unfortunately for me, his first attempt at affection is scratching. Did you know that baby fingernails are like claws? So around I walk with scars of affection on my face. They hurt, but no hurt has ever been better.

It would be easy for me to just not let my son get close to my face. I'd save both my appearance and my nerve endings. But I'd miss out on that smile. I'd be keeping my son from learning how to love me. I'd be keeping him from expressing the love he was designed to express. So I bear the scars of affection, both because it is beautiful and because it's a part of my son's healthy development.

SCARRED BY AFFECTION

That's all sort of cute and such, but it's almost not fair. It's not fair because it's a tiny sacrifice for someone I love beyond description.[1] What about the love that reaps real physical harm?

Around the year 250 A.D., a plague of smallpox struck the whole Roman Empire. Healthy people were evacuated from cities, while the sick were left to die alone. Cyprian, a Christian bishop in North Africa, instructed his congregants to stay in the cities and wash the wounds of the dying. At the same time, the empire was blaming the Christians for the plague. It was a popular notion that the gods caused the plague because they were angry that Christianity had been allowed to spread. This notion ignited one of the most thorough and violent persecutions of Christians in Roman history. So it is entirely possible and likely that the sick people Christians cared for were folks who believed the plague was the result of Christianity. Some accounts say that the Christian caretakers died while their patients got better. They washed wounds, provided food and water, prayed, and even properly buried those who died. They literally gave their lives in love for their enemy. The scars on my nose seem pretty small now, don't you think?

You might read that and think, "Oh, what a tragedy!" Yet the Christian voices of the time describe this experience with sacred joy. They were happy to live God's love. They knew Christ had died for them and they were ecstatic to be able to offer a similar sacrifice to their neighbor; even if that neighbor hated them. They died not with the scars of tragedy, but the scars of affection.

I write all this to point out that Jesus doesn't promise that loving your enemies will be peachy. It got him killed.

---

1. Or, in the words of Jesus: "If you love those who love you, what credit is that to you? For even sinners love those who love them" (Luke 6:32, NRSV).

But death, in Christianity, doesn't mean failure—it means hope. Just like my scars empower my son to grow and learn and just like the scars of the ancient caretaking Christians produced joy, so too when we venture out in love for those who would do us harm, God brings life, hope, forgiveness, and reconciliation. I think our world and our neighborhoods need that kind of self-giving love. I think we have to overcome the fear of what it will cost us to love our communities, our crazy uncle, the beggar on the corner, or the politician we despise. I think we have to be willing to be wounded by our affection for the world around us. And I can't wait to see what lively joy God shall bring from the scars.

10

Which Jesus?

"Why do you call me 'Lord, Lord', and do not do what I tell you? I will show you what someone is like who comes to me, hears my words, and acts on them. That one is like a man building a house, who dug deeply and laid the foundation on rock; when a flood arose, the river burst against that house but could not shake it, because it had been well built. But the one who hears and does not act is like a man who built a house on the ground without a foundation. When the river burst against it, immediately it fell, and great was the ruin of that house."

LUKE 6:46-49 (NRSV)

WHEN MY WIFE AND I were shopping for a house a few years ago, there were a lot of cool, cheap homes for sale. One home in particular stuck out to us as a great deal for its unique and beautiful setting. It was an old Victorian home with an incredible garden for a backyard. On the top story stood a balcony off the main bedroom, perfect for morning coffee. A breakfast nook gave us images of lazy Saturday mornings reading the paper and joking with our kids. It was like a dream. It also did not have a foundation. It turns out banks won't give people money for houses without foundations. They're cash-only deals. Banks know that a home without a proper foundation is a huge risk. If the buyer ever defaults on their loan then the bank is stuck with a pretty worthless/useless/unlivable home. The foundation is what gives a home its ability to serve its purpose through storms, slides, earthquakes, floods, etc. Despite the Victorian dream home's ability to fill our mind with comforting visions, its lack of a foundation made it dangerous to us physically and financially.

So what's the church's foundation? Doctrine? Theological detail? Worship style? Sermon eloquence? Creativity? Trendiness? Coffee in the lobby? Khakis or jeans or skirts? Politics? Much like the rooms in a home, these things can fill us with dreams, but without a solid undergirding they are quite dangerous to live in. I can't prove this, but it seems to me that communities founded on any of the above crumble in hardship (or at least lose touch with their purpose). I mean, no one is giving up their life for jeans, right? I, for one, will never be a martyr for Chris Tomlin, Matt Redman, or Charles Wesley.

But for Jesus, what would we endure for Jesus? Against which of life's bursting waters would we stand well-built? The church standing on the words of Jesus has, indeed, endured many storms. Roman paranoia-driven persecution; millennia of doctrinal violence; deep divisiveness; Dark Ages; corrupt priests; bloody, unholy crusades; war-causing reformations; colonization; slavery; secularization; and worship wars. In each generation some leaders choose to hold onto power during the storm and for a while they seem to be the ones who prosper. But eventually they and

Which Jesus?

their followers crumble under the weight of their own deceit. Then time reveals a precious few who labored day and night, often at the risk of their lives, to build a church devoted to Jesus.[1] Yes, the church of segregationists prospered in the 1950s, but then when it crumbled we learned the stories of freedom churches who had peacefully stood their ground during the South's swelling storm. So, though history is filled with many violent squalls the church that stands is the one whose foundation rests on Christ. It seems that for Jesus some would stand to the very end.

But which Jesus? "Buddy Jesus?" Liberal Jesus? Conservative Jesus? American Jesus? Jewish Jesus? Poor Jesus? Rich Jesus? Racist Jesus? Smorgasbord Jesus? Flavor-of-the-month Jesus? Church of God Jesus? Catholic Jesus? Orthodox Jesus? The words we add to Jesus are powerfully dubious. Overtime the allure of the adjective becomes far more consequential to us than Jesus himself. The adjectives themselves become our sandy foundations. And when the flood comes disaster is had. In many ways, this is the point of this book. We as individuals and we as the church have to do the hard earthmoving work to make sure that all is resting on Jesus and his way. When you build a foundation you have to excavate, digging into bedrock. You also must use the strongest, most trustworthy material available to you for the foundation. Thus, we must search deep within the Gospels to learn as much about Jesus as possible. I want a church and a faith founded on nothing less than Jesus. So which Jesus? How about beginning with the Jesus that Luke is sketching for us?

---

1. For examples of Christians doing great work while the church's leaders prospered unethically, consider Saint Francis during the Crusades, the Beguines and Beghards under corrupt Popes, or the Jesuits' work in South America during colonization.

The Upside Down Way

- Humble (6:17–19)
- Compassionate (everywhere)
- Patient (6:17–19)
- Suffers real human experiences (4:1–30)
- Uninterested in fame or power (4:9–13)
- Loves enemies (6:27–36)
- Dignifies, includes, and empowers the forgotten and ostracized (4:31–41; 5:12–14, 17–25, 27–32; 6:6–11)
- Heals without prejudice (6:19)
- Heals physically, spiritually, emotionally, and socially (5:12–14)
- Authoritative (4:32)
- Rejected (4:16–30)
- Carves out time to be alone, but patiently loves those who interrupt him (4:42; 6:12)
- People and their needs are more important than religious traditions (5:12–26; 6:1–11)
- Forgiving, merciful (5:17–26)
- Looking for Kingdom-learners (5:1–11; 6:12–19)
- Good news for the broken (6:20–23)
- Bad news for the self-sufficient (6:24–26)
- Parties with sinners (5:27–32)

That Jesus.

May your life proceed from such a well-built foundation. And may the church build itself on nothing more or less than Jesus.

11

Where Is Your Faith?

One day he got into a boat with his disciples, and he said to them, "Let us go across to the other side of the lake." So they put out, and while they were sailing he fell asleep. A gale swept down on the lake, and the boat was filling with water, and they were in danger. They went to him and woke him up, shouting, "Master, Master, we are perishing!" And he woke up and rebuked the wind and the raging waves; they ceased, and there was a calm. He said to them, "Where is your faith?" They were afraid and amazed, and said to one another, "Who then is this, that he commands even the winds and the water, and they obey him?"

LUKE 8:22–25 (NRSV)

"WHERE IS YOUR FAITH?" Compassionate words for such a time, don't you think? Is Jesus so calloused as to dismiss the gravity of a dangerous storm on the Sea of Galilee? Is he unconcerned with our misfortune? With our storms and dangers?

The Upside Down Way

I'm guessing the disciples didn't venture out onto the sea in bad weather. In fact, the Sea of Galilee is famous for fickle weather. Maybe they had no warning. Maybe they were looking forward to a beautiful day on the lake. Maybe one moment they were basking in the warm sun and the next they were bailing water from the hull. In any regard, the dark clouds and grave winds descended upon them and threatened to submerge their otherwise happy vessel.

So why does Jesus get testy with them? Perhaps because Jesus won't always be asleep in the boat. A day will come when these very men won't be saved from the tumults of life. They'll be dragged, beaten, imprisoned, crucified, boiled, and reviled. The waters of life will rise around them and no words, beautiful or profound, will make it go calm. They'll need something to get them through the storm (think about Luke 6:46–49 in the previous devotion).

And that's really the point of faith. It doesn't always change our circumstances, but it does get us through. It doesn't always make waters placid, but it is strong in the storm. It keeps your spirit afloat. It reminds you that, though he be hard to see, Jesus *is* in the storm too. Faith keeps your eyes fixed on him. Faith compels you to follow him in life's dark straits; to keep loving, forgiving, healing, seeking, listening, giving, and hoping.

So, ask yourself today, "Where's my faith?"

12

Fear in the Way

Then Jesus called the twelve together and gave them power and authority over all demons and to cure diseases, and he sent them out to proclaim the kingdom of God and to heal. He said to them, "Take nothing for your journey, no staff, nor bag, nor bread, nor money –not even an extra tunic. Whatever house you enter, stay there, and leave from there. Wherever they do not welcome you, as you are leaving that town shake the dust off your feet as a testimony against them." They departed and went through the villages, bringing the good news and curing diseases everywhere.

LUKE 9:1–6 (NRSV)

WHEN I WAS A child I remember singing a song at church that said something along the lines of, "Wherever you send me, I will go." That line always unsettled my spirit. I kind of liked my life and if I were to leave I preferred it be on my own terms. When we'd get to that part of the song my volume would decrease; eventually, I just wouldn't sing it at all. Instead of singing, I would often feel visceral fear accompanied by terrifying questions: *Is God really going to pluck me out of Indiana and send me somewhere I don't want to go? Am I Jonah?* The song was just one instance of this, it seemed like every other Sunday had something to do with God sending us all somewhere. Missionary veneration is a practice woven deeply into the consciousness of Evangelical Christianity. The storyline goes something like this: *let me show you a good example of what it looks like to follow Jesus; God called so-and-so away from a great job to the far stretches of the Hinterland; and so-and-so went without question.* The implication is that if you really want to follow God then you'll do the same. The assumption is that God does want you to follow him, so eventually he'll call you to the Hinterland too.[1] Thus, my fear seemed pretty logical.

Then I got to college and discovered that I wasn't the only young Christian who thought God was planning to mercilessly uproot me from my happy life and send me to some unpleasant hostile land. All the guys in my Bible study agreed that sooner or later it was going to happen. The pious among us were preparing for the bravery to say yes, while the cowardly, I among them, were looking for a fishing vessel en route to Tarshish.

When you get to texts like Luke 9:1–6 you too might feel that gnawing fear that God's going to send you into the middle of nowhere, no car, nor smart phone, nor backpack, nor debit card, not even an extra pair of pants.

Fear, in this case, is a huge distraction.

Notice that this passage never says that Jesus said, "And let every good churchgoer do exactly what you have

---

1. A worse option: if being a missionary is the highest Christian pursuit then what does that say about God's view of you if he doesn't call you? I know more than a few Christians who live with the kind of shame that derives from this line of thinking.

done."[2] The idea that God is constantly sending the holy from Timbuktu to Joppa to Seattle really messes with our interpretation of scripture. Jonah is the clearest instance of this. Think about the way we typically tell Jonah's story: *God calls Jonah; Jonah gets scared and runs away; God gets mad and punishes Jonah by having a fish swallow him; Jonah repents, the fish vomits; Jonah, like a good Christian, goes where God told him.* I can't tell you how many times the retelling of Jonah's story stops there. But read the following words carefully:

> When God saw what they did, how they turned from their evil ways, God changed his mind about the calamity that he had said he would bring upon them; and he did not do it. But this was very displeasing to Jonah, and he became angry. He prayed to the Lord and said, "O Lord! Is not this what I said while I was still in my own country? *That is why I fled to Tarshish at the beginning; for I knew that you are a gracious God and merciful, slow to anger, and abounding in steadfast love, and ready to relent from punishing* (Jonah 3:10—4:2, NRSV; my emphasis).

Jonah didn't go to Nineveh because he knew God planned to be gracious to the Ninevites! I know the word racist gets tossed about in our world, but if ever there were a fitting place for it! Jonah should be an awesome story about God's deep desire to be merciful to every nation and tribe on his planet. But because of our preoccupation with and fear of sending we've really lost the heart of it. All we can see in Jonah is our own proclivity to run away from what scares us. We read a merciless, missionary-plucker God into Jonah's

---

2. I can't think of any passage that makes traveling holier than staying at home. If Jesus can't be followed in both places then he can't be followed.

story when the writer of Jonah has gone to great lengths to elevate the boundless mercy of this God above all other notions. Our fear isn't just a distraction. It is a muddler of the text of scripture.

So Luke's words, fear aside, what *are* they about? Well, one thing that strikes me is the last line. These first Christ-followers proclaimed Jesus' lordship. They *also* dove into the very real and very present physical needs of those they encountered along the way. It seems to me that those two "poles" of ministry are essential. It is so easy to do one at the expense of the other. We have a message about Christ the King. We also have the resources that would allow us to be beneficial, even healing, to people in desperate need. To accomplish both it will take a dependence upon the Spirit, a radical love for both Christ and all types people, a boldness not of our own, wide open ears, and not a small amount of humility. And, unless God specifically tells you otherwise, it won't require gas in your car, plane tickets, bug spray, or walking any further than across the street.

13

Breaking Down the Kitchen Door

Now as they went on their way, he entered a certain village, where a woman named Martha welcomed him into her home. She had a sister named Mary, who sat at the Lord's feet and listened to what he was saying. But Martha was distracted by her many tasks; so she came to him and asked, "Lord, do you not care that my sister has left me to do all the work by myself? Tell her then to help me." But the Lord answered her, "Martha, Martha, you are worried and distracted by many things; there is need of only one thing. Mary has chosen the better part, which will not be taken away from her."

LUKE 10:38–42 (NRSV)

HAVE YOU EVER BEEN stuck in a room? I had a babysitter once who had a room that she kept all of us kids in. It wasn't too small or unclean or unsafe, but it was kind of small and filled with girls' toys. The room had big windows that looked out into the backyard. I know the babysitter meant well. She just wanted to give us a safe place, all our own. Instead, I found the room suffocating. I was a child who spent every waking moment outside running around. In this room I couldn't run, I couldn't be active, and as far as I was concerned that meant I couldn't be me. So rather than making the best of it, I would just sit with my face pressed up against the window, wishing I could run and roll in the grass.

One day the sun was out, the air was warm, and there were only a few kids to babysit so she let us play in the backyard. I was the first kid out the door. I can still remember running around her garden, the sun on my cheeks, my heart beating hard, and an ineffable sense that this is what it means to be alive.

Our world's history is filled with rooms that people were stuck in—often rooms of violence and oppression: African Americans shackled in the room of slavery; Jews taken from their home because of the room of paranoia and destroyed in the hate-mortared rooms of concentration camps; Christians bludgeoned in the room of martyrdom; or untouchables unable to move in the room of India's caste system. Other rooms are not so well defined; the walls are made from the expectations of the powerful and the biases of the ignorant. Like the small kid who gets picked last for playground games because small and athletic are in two different rooms; the homeless man who gets turned away from a well-to-do church because piety can't possibly be pungent or poor; the young black man who is pulled over because he is black; or the first-century Palestinian woman whose room is the kitchen.

Jewish women didn't get to learn from Rabbis. Jewish women certainly didn't get to sit at the feet of a teacher. Jewish women had a place, a room: the kitchen. Martha isn't mad because there is work to be done, she's mad because Mary is out of place. Jesus is over for dinner and that means the old boundaries, the old traditions, the old gender roles are insufficient. Jesus is new wine, and Martha wants to use an old wineskin. Mary, on the other hand, understands what's happening. Jesus is an open door to sunlight and freedom. She's getting caught up in the kingdom of God, ready to move with it and wanting to prepare as an agent of it. That room of flour, bowls, fire, and fish is too small for what's going on inside her. Because of Jesus she can't be content to be what her society has told her she has to be. Sitting at Jesus' feet isn't just about bending her knees and submitting to gravity, it's about breaking down the kitchen door to follow Jesus.[1]

So, what's your room?

In case you have one (or more), I hear that Jesus is a room liberator.[2]

---

1. For more on the historical background of this passage see, Wright, *Luke*, 129–32.

2. Sometimes liberation doesn't come in the form of a literal wall falling down. I think about the millions of men, women, and children who died as slaves in the American South. They never saw that sunshine of freedom. But Jesus didn't leave them unliberated. Jesus, for many of them, liberated their minds so that they found freedom in the clinch of slavery's shackles. That is not to diminish the evil of slavery, but to laud the perseverance of those women, men, and children and to praise Jesus for not leaving them to darkness.

14

Money, Health, and Striving

"And do not keep striving for what you are to eat and what you are to drink, and do not keep worrying. For it is the nations of the world that strive after all these things, and your Father knows that you need them. Instead, strive for his kingdom, and these things will be given to you as well."

LUKE 12:29-31 (NIV)

WRITING ABOUT MONEY IS always controversial. There are bound to be disagreements over what follows. So let me say this first: I don't think I have the right to tell you how much money you should make and how much you should give away. As with anything, I think it is more important that our hearts be shaped by Jesus' kingdom of love than that we follow a formula.[1] That's why "tithe-talk" in the Church agitates me. Tithe-talk typically centers on one verse:

---

1. As Jesus says to the Pharisees when they're following a legal formula: "So give for alms [offerings to the poor] those things that are within; and see, everything will be clean for you" (Luke 11:41, NRSV).

> "Bring the whole tithe into the storehouse, that there may be food in my house. Test me in this," says the Lord Almighty, "and see if I will not throw open the floodgates of heaven and pour out so much blessing that there will not be room enough to store it" (Mal 3:10, NIV).

From there we often create a mathematical formula for stewardship: give 10 percent, keep 90 percent, and expect God to mysteriously put more resources in our laps. What's the problem with that? A few suggestions:

a. It creates the attitude that we're entitled to ninety percent.
b. It suggests that we give for the sake of getting.
c. It does not take into account what God said that the tithe was to be used for.[2]
d. It assumes that this is all the Bible has to say about money. Or is used as an excuse to ignore whatever else the Bible does say—and boy, does it say some things.
e. Finally, where's the love? Tithing, as it has been taught to me, can be accomplished without any regard for Jesus' loving kingdom. I'm not too interested in teaching anything that doesn't require love.[3]

---

[2]. See Deut 14:22–27. One has to ask, if the offering isn't being used to support widows, foreigners, orphans, and the poor, is the money really a tithe?

[3]. I don't want to undo tithing. I think ten percent (which is all "tithe" means) is a fine suggestion for anyone who wants a benchmark. All I want to point out is, absent love, tithing is just a clanging offering plate. Consider Luke 11:42 "But woe to you Pharisees! For you tithe the mint and rue and herbs of all kinds, and neglect justice and the love of God; it is these you ought to have practiced, without neglecting the others" (NRSV). Really, I hope I'm not doing anything more here than echoing Jesus' sentiment.

The Upside Down Way

What am I interested in? A needs-based approach to money and resources. This is an expansive topic that deserves its own book-length discussion.[4] Therefore, understand that what follows only scratches the surface. It is my opinion that the purpose of money (and all our resources) is to meet needs. Jesus, in the passage I cited to begin with, tells us to not strive for possessions (even basic ones). He doesn't say, *don't try at all to use your money to clothe your children*. Or, *don't lift a finger to provide for your basic needs*. He does center in on where our striving leads. Have we offered our resources to the striving of Jesus' generous kingdom? Or have we retained our energy for our own striving's sake? Jesus seems to be concerned with how much energy we devote to provision; not with dissuading his followers from devoting any energy to it. He has just told a parable about a man who strove to accumulate massive amounts of wealth—it seems that Luke 12:29–31 is a commentary/explanation of that parable (Lk. 12:13–21). Money, therefore, is not for accumulation. Money is not for ostentation. Money is not for glory. Money is not for personal excess, even if you have given the church a cut of your first fruits. Money is a means for meeting our needs and for the furtherance of Jesus' vision(s). That's why the state of monetary allocation in our world is so egregious. A few people have way more than they need and a whole lot of people have way less than they need.[5]

Need is a complicated noun. Food, water, and shelter are basic and universally recognized as needs. But I think

---

4. For an excellent book-length resource see Foster, *Freedom of Simplicity*.

5. Ten percent of the world owns 85 percent of the resources. See Davies, "The Global Distribution of Household Wealth." Meanwhile, eighteen thousand children die every day from preventable diseases. For more, see Sider, *Rich Christians*, 3.

humans have been created with a lot more needs than the basic three. We need dignity, community, self-esteem, pleasure, fun, joy, hope, art/creativity, love, solitude, work, purpose, and (fill in your own suggestion here).[6] Need can be a synonym for what it takes to survive, but I prefer to think about needs in terms of health. If you're on a desert island, but have ample food, water, and shelter then your body will keep breathing, but what of your mind, heart, and soul? Thus, survival and health are not synonyms. Survival is a purely physical matter; health is a matter of wholeness.

The Bible begins with a grand story about how God created a beautiful world designed to provide a system of health for all his creatures (Gen 1–2).[7] Consider that God created the stars as servants, tasked with communicating the seasons to humans (Gen 1:14–16). Or that humans were created as servants tasked with caring for God's creation (Gen 1:28–30, 2:15). God designed creatures and resources to benefit and meet the needs of others. When we hoard we rob God's world of its design. When we don't meet our kids' needs for security and self-worth we fail at one of our most basic responsibilities. When we have an unutilized resource it's like we've dug a hole and put it in the ground.[8] When we forget about the massively under-served masses we misuse what's been entrusted to us.

---

6. Clearly money won't buy us all these things, but it can be used in support of these things.

7. For more on this system of health in Genesis see Goldingay, *Old Testament Theology*, Vol. 1, 42–130.

8. This is actually a fantastic practical question: *what do we have that isn't being used?* And, *how can we use it to benefit someone's needs?* As the pastor of a church with a small budget this question has given us tremendous opportunities to have an impact on our community beyond our monetary reach. For instance, we have an empty room at the church that we allow a local non-profit thrift store to use as storage.

The Upside Down Way

In other words, let's use our money to strike a balance between meeting our needs, our family's, our community's, and the world's. Oh, and let's do it because our hearts are bent on *striving* for Jesus' kingdom.

15

Marching up the Hill

And the Lord said, "Who then is the faithful and prudent manager whom his master will put in charge of his slaves, to give them their allowance of food at the proper time? Blessed is that slave whom his master will find at work when he arrives. Truly I tell you, he will put that one in charge of all his possessions. But if that slave says to himself, 'My master is delayed in coming,' and if he begins to beat the other slaves, men and women, and to eat and drink and get drunk, the master of that slave will come on a day when he does not expect him and at an hour that he does not know, and will cut him in pieces, and put him with the unfaithful. That slave who knew what his master wanted, but did not prepare himself or do what was wanted, will receive a severe beating.

LUKE 12:42–47 (NRSV)

BEFORE WE GET TO Jesus and his stern warning, I'd like to ask you to read another set of poetic and prophetic words:

The Upside Down Way

> In a sense we have come to our nation's capital to cash a check. When the architects of our republic wrote the magnificent words of the Constitution and the Declaration of Independence, they were signing a promissory note to which every American was to fall heir. This note was a promise that all men, yes, black men as well as white men, would be guaranteed the unalienable rights of life, liberty, and the pursuit of happiness. It is obvious today that America has defaulted on this promissory note insofar as her citizens of color are concerned. Instead of honoring this sacred obligation, America has given the Negro people a bad check, a check which has come back marked "insufficient funds." But we refuse to believe that the bank of justice is bankrupt.[1]

Martin Luther King Jr. spoke these words as the conclusion of an historic march on the nation's capital. He stood in the shadow of the great emancipator, Abraham Lincoln. He spoke as an heir of the ideals of Lincoln and our country's founders, as a prophet of the Declaration of Independence, and a preacher of the Constitution. He had marched on Washington with his compatriots to bring charges against the nation's lawmakers—the curators of America's liberty.

At this point in Luke, Jesus too is marching; marching up toward Zion's holy hill. He's on his way to the curators of God's temple. He's on his way to the watchmen of God's presence, the servants God left in charge. And how will he find them? Like Washington in the 1960s? A bureaucratic body bent on providing services for some and not services for others? Or, as intended, a house of prayer for all nations?[2]

---

1. King, Jr., "I Have a Dream."
2. See Isa 56:3–7.

Marching up the Hill

This chapter in Luke is often interpreted as warnings for the end of time. That may very well be—biblical passages are often about more than one thing. Yet, I think it is a mistake to forget what these words mean in the arc of Luke's storyline.[3] These are words of warning to Jerusalem and the established religious leadership.[4] When Jesus arrives in Jerusalem he goes straight to the temple (Luke 19:44–45). Jews believed that the temple was the literal footstool of God's throne, an intersection of heaven and earth. Their religious practices were designed to keep certain people away from God's presence and allow "special" groups of people closer access. The temple had also become intertwined with the local economy in a way that was especially hard on the poor.[5] What was supposed to be the bank of God's presence had become a spiritual Ponzi scheme. The servants in charge were hurting the poor, "containing" the presence of God, and getting drunk on power, tradition, and wine.

The great irony is that while the temple priests worked so hard to keep the presence of God secured behind curtains and towers, God is about to come in the front door. He's on his way home and will turn the tables on the servants in charge. He'll announce judgment on them and their system. And he'll raise himself up as the final sacrifice,

---

3. Luke 9:51 reads, "When the days drew near for him to be taken up, he set his face to go to Jerusalem" (NRSV). From this point onward in Luke, Jesus is quite literally on a march to Jerusalem.

4. Jesus is much more explicit about the warnings and their connection to Jerusalem when some Pharisees tip him off that Herod is plotting his assassination. See Luke 13:31–35. It is also more explicit in Luke 20:9–19, especially verse 19.

5. Jesus calls the temple a "den of robbers" in Luke 19:46 and then denounces the scribes, who were in charge of the temple tax, for getting rich off the offerings of impoverished widows (Luke 20:45—21:4).

becoming himself the way by which people relate to God.[6] He'll cash God's promissory note for his presence with or without the religious leaders of the day.

And we, of course, are keepers of that message. We are a community of Jesus' servants charged with feeding people, taking care of people, working on behalf of God's vision for humanity, and proclaiming the message that God wants a relationship with everyone through Jesus. We're the servants left in charge. When the Master comes, how will he find us?

---

6. See John 2:18–22.

16

Swallow Jesus?

Now large crowds were traveling with him; and he turned and said to them, "Whoever comes to me and does not hate father and mother, wife and children, brothers and sisters, yes, and even life itself, cannot be my disciple. Whoever does not carry the cross and follow me cannot be my disciple. For which of you, intending to build a tower, does not first sit down and estimate the cost, to see whether he has enough to complete it? Otherwise, when he has laid a foundation and is not able to finish, all who see it will begin to ridicule him, saying, 'This fellow began to build and was not able to finish.' Or what king, going out to wage war against another king, will not sit down first and consider whether he is able with ten thousand to oppose the one who comes against him with twenty thousand? If he cannot, then, while the other is still far away, he sends a delegation and asks for the terms of peace. So therefore, none of you can become my disciple if you do not give up all your possessions.

LUKE 14:25–33 (NRSV)

The Upside Down Way

ALMOST EVERY ALTAR CALL I've ever witnessed has been the same message: you've done something to screw your life up, you need to tell God, and if you tell him sincerely and publicly he'll make it better.[1] This particular formula, colored by variations in images, stories, and vocabulary, is almost exclusively the message for the big Christian gatherings I've attended. I like to call the overuse of this approach "medicinal salvation"—in other words, the point of the Christian life is to feel better.[2] Now, I definitely believe that God has the power to do incredible things in our lives. I think there is a time and place for people to experience healing that only God can offer. And I wholeheartedly believe that God cares deeply about our wellbeing. However, wellbeing and feeling good are not equivalents. Healing and euphoria, too, are not equals. One of the biggest pitfalls of medicinal salvation is that it makes Jesus a pill you take. Show up to this sermon, swallow/digest Jesus, and experience the immediate benefits. Instead, discipleship is a process, a slow-release transformation. It's more like carrying a cross than swallowing a pill.

I fear that when we read, "carry your cross," we don't grasp what Jesus is saying. Imagine proclaiming in the old West, "Tie your own noose and follow me." Or "Gather your own firing squad!" "Plug in your own electric chair," so on and so forth. The people who first heard this had probably seen a crucifixion. Romans would crucify rebels and leave

---

1. The altar call is fairly young in the history of the church. It started with the revivalist preacher Charles Finney around 1825 in NYC. The method by which Christians respond to sermons has always been unique to the time and culture of the parishioners. I wonder if it is again time for us to re-imagine a response that better fits our current culture.

2. For further clarification, I'm not anti-medicine. It's all a matter of dosage; much the same as a medicinal overdose, this approach done out of balance can lead to an incapacitated church.

their bodies to decompose along prominent routes—a warning of the consequences of opposition to Rome. I don't know how or why anyone kept following Jesus after such grim predictions. But, at least they couldn't accuse Jesus of filling their heads with images of grandeur. At least he was upfront. What gets me is why we aren't upfront? I've known so many people and read so many authors who go to tremendous lengths to diminish the cost of following Jesus. Again, it can be like Jesus is a hallucinogenic drug, ingested by prayer, provided by biblical dealers, and taken en masse at every service and rally in order to alter believers' glum realities.[3]

Back to Luke: Jesus is on his way to Jerusalem, where he'll be tried, beaten, flogged, mocked, and pegged to a rough-hewn cross.[4] The people he is addressing are on Jerusalem's road *with him*. If they intended to stick with him to the end (you might remember Peter's promise, "Lord, I am ready to go with you to prison and to death!" [Lk. 22:33b]) they'd have to let go of family ties, worldly accomplishments, and possessions. They'd have to settle for being left with nothing but Jesus and the cross. Of course, no one did that. They left him to a cross all his own.

> "Jesus has always many who love His heavenly kingdom, but few who bear His cross. He has many who desire consolation, but few who care for trial. He finds many to share His table, but few

---

3. Some Christian traditions have made a living off of the prosperity Gospel (Jesus = health and wealth), but I'm not just talking about that. It is my sense that a lot of Christians my age have abandoned the Evangelical Church because of what I am talking about—a shallow, feel-good Gospel. Again, I'm not saying that Jesus doesn't care about "glum realities." I think he cares deeply. I just take issue with equating Jesus' care with the whole of the Gospel. The whole of the Gospel includes Christian mission, which will sometimes feel like a splintery cross.

4. Trust me, they did not smooth the logs with sandpaper.

to take part in His fasting. All desire to be happy with Him; few wish to suffer anything for Him."[5]

I wrote previously that these biblical passages aren't simply barricaded in the first century. There is a point for the people who heard the words from Jesus' lips *and* a point for those who would follow him now. I want to follow Jesus. We want to follow Jesus. So, what does it mean for us? Two suggestions:

a. Eventually Jesus is going to call us to walk Golgotha's lonely hill with him: the price of a hotel room for a homeless family; a trip to a faraway place without your family's approval; a relationship with an outcast; an addict who needs your encouragement and presence; a moment when we need to admit we were wrong. These moments sharpen our gaze on Christ and his road. We forsake even the basics of life because a hurting person needs us to follow Jesus. For 90 percent of us, these are temporary sacrifices. Nevertheless, the time(s) comes.

b. There are also more continuous crosses to bear: the person who annoys you at work; the family member who's left your relationship; the depression that stalks you like a shadow; addiction (because you're always an addict, even when you're not using); doubts; unfulfilled dreams; exhaustion; the lingering pain of tragedy; or the bitterness of betrayal. The question is, in the midst of these situations will we pick up the cross and walk in Jesus' direction? The direction of grace, mercy, reconciliation, humility, love, justice, truth, and generosity.

So, consider this a call to the altar at Golgotha's base: where's your cross and are you ready to pick it up?

5. Thomas à Kempis, *The Imitation of Christ*, 39. Thomas à Kempis was a fifteenth-century monk who transcribed this old monastic rule. It's famous for its frank recommendation that Christians should suffer for Christ; not easy stuff to swallow.

17

Yours or Ours?

But he answered his father, "Listen! For all these years I have been working like a slave for you, and I have never disobeyed your command; yet you have never given me even a young goat so that I might celebrate with my friends. But when *this son of yours* came back, who has devoured your property with prostitutes, you killed the fatted calf for him!" Then the father said to him, "Son, you are always with me, and all that is mine is yours. But we had to celebrate and rejoice, because *this brother of yours* was dead and has come to life; he was lost and has been found."

LUKE 15:29–32 (NRSV, MY EMPHASIS)

EXCLUSION AND INCLUSION ARE big words in our culture today. In fact, I hesitate to use them, lest their baggage draw my writing away from the intended point. But they are exactly what the end of Jesus' *Prodigal Son* parable is about. I've highlighted two key and related phrases for you: "This son of yours" and "This brother of yours." Keep these opposing perspectives in mind.

For about five years now I've spent a lot of time pondering the Lord's Prayer (Luke 11:2–4). There are a lot of reasons for that, but the one pertinent to this discussion is the word, "our."

Our heavenly Father . . .
Our daily bread . . .
Our debts . . .

Not mine. Not yours. Not Israel's.[1] Not Democrats'. Not Seattle Seahawks fans'. Not successful people's. Ours. *We* are a global species made of a whole lot of different types. But at, or at least near, the center of the Christian message is the belief that we all have one Father and we're all brothers and sisters. You can waste your divine inheritance on a myriad of destructive practices, but you're always Abba's child and I'm always your brother.

Jesus' elder son character is trying to distance himself from his younger brother. With his language the older brother disowns, or at least diminishes, his blood-bond to the squanderer. He is also claiming that by his devout behavior he is so different from the younger son that they're essentially not of the same family. The Father deftly reminds him of their relationship . . . their closeness. It is the Father's prerogative to keep them aware of their interconnectedness; to try, by grace, to hold the family together. Because inclusion in the family isn't a matter of hard work and following the rules, inclusion in the family is a matter

---

1. See Wright, *Luke*, 190. Wright argues that the Pharisees who opposed Jesus are almost certainly in view when Jesus creates the older brother. These Pharisees made a living off of sorting out who was really a member of the people of God and who wasn't. Too often, their criteria for inclusion had to do with money, purity, success, and devotion to Torah. If they had said the words, "Our Father," they would have only been thinking about law-abiding Jewish males.

of one's relationship to the Father. Claim him as your Father and you're included. Exclusion, then, isn't something that the family does to people—the older son can't say, *he can be your son, but not my brother!* Exclusion is something that sons and daughters choose by abandoning the Father.

But let's be honest, the Church takes it as one of its primary objectives to proclaim who is excluded. Rather than pointing people to our common Father, we over-examine what makes one group of people different from another group of people. If you know a non-Christian don't beleaguer your conversation with matters of ethics, for instance. The person doesn't need to know how different they are from you because they sleep around or meditate on Buddha's path. What they need to know is that you share a common Father, who is desperately awaiting a renewed relationship with them and has made it possible through Jesus. If God is indeed God, he'll set to shaping their morality as a result of their relationship.[2] Our job is to point people toward the loving God revealed through Jesus. Not to meticulously sort them into camps like "us" and "them."

N.T. Wright points out the great irony of the older brother's desire to differentiate himself from the younger:

---

2. Certainly the Church should be involved in the process. I don't think transformation happens in isolation. I think the Church stands in a peculiar place of advantage when it comes to creating a space for life-transformation. But it ever astounds me how Christians want the life-transformation to happen *before* people embrace Jesus. So many launch into the public sphere with moral arguments and expect people who don't believe in Jesus to quickly adopt Jesus' moral yoke regardless of whether those same people have a relationship with Jesus. A glaring example of this today is the way Evangelical Christians often approach the issue of homosexuality. It comes across to my ears as, "We don't care what you think about Jesus, just please don't be a homosexual anymore." The more we harp on morality outside the context of a transforming relationship with Jesus, the less opportunity we will have to actually talk to people about Jesus.

> The older brother shows, in his bad temper, that he has had no more real respect for his father than his brother had had. He lectures him in front of his guests, and refuses his plea to come in. Once more the father is generous, this time to his self-righteous older son.[3]

In other words, the difference is in his head. He's decided that the debauchery of his brother is worse than his pride. That leaving haughtily is worse than staying stubbornly. The truth is my pride is as destructive a force as alcoholism. My greed can bring down a home or society as quickly as fornication. So if you want to talk about ethics with wayward sons and daughters focus on the similarity of your brokenness and the sweetness of reforming grace in your life.

Can we refrain from the older brother's divisive relationship parsing? Or is this legacy of the church too ingrained? Too human? I think and I hope that there is room still to allow his Spirit to grow us out of "this son of yours" and into "Our Father."

---

3. Wright, *Luke*, 191.

18

Include Lazarus

There was a certain rich man, which was clothed in purple and fine linen, and fared sumptuously every day: and there was a certain beggar named Lazarus, which was laid at his gate, full of sores, and desiring to be fed with the crumbs which fell from the rich man's table: moreover the dogs came and licked his sores. And it came to pass, that the beggar died, and was carried by the angels into Abraham's bosom: the rich man also died, and was buried; and in hell he lift up his eyes, being in torments, and seeth Abraham afar off, and Lazarus in his bosom.

LUKE 16:19−23(AKJV)

Lazarus

LAZARUS MEANS, "GOD IS my help."

We have forty Jesus-parables in the Gospels and this is the only time that Jesus names one of his characters. I take that to mean Lazarus is pretty significant.

I've had the privilege of meeting a lot of Lazaruses in my life. And one of the things that always strikes me about men and women who are covered with life-sores and beg as a means of sustenance is that they're dying to tell their story. Sometimes the sores are so deep that they tell an imaginary story about themselves, because at the center of their being they believe their real story isn't worth mentioning. The saddest situation is when a person has been so picked at by life that they've given up on telling their story at all. They sit, perhaps, at the same gate every day, voiceless and invisible; they long to be included, even if only the way a dog is included in a family gathering or a feast (eating the crumbs that fall from the table). In reality, they sit paralyzed from a pervasive inner voice, "I am worthless."

Ministry to Lazarus then has little to do with food.[1] If we want to minister to Lazarus we have to jump into the pit of his self-despair. We have to listen to his story, historical or fantastical, to show him that he's included; that we see him and hear him. We have to set up a table, a feast, invite him as a member of the family, and spoil him with our attention and love. We'd have to leave no doubt in his mind that he was included. Maybe we'd invite him to work in the yard with us, to sing a song, to go for a walk, to read the bible, to eat ice cream in the grass, to laugh at a table of friends, or to chat over a steaming cup of coffee. And perhaps, our work to include him would give him a ladder out of the pit.[2]

---

1. Although, to ignore his bare needs of clothing, food, and medicine would be inhumane.

2. I'm trying to be poetic, but I should also admit the pit of self-despair is not an easy pit to escape. It can take years and years. I know a man who walked steadily with a young couple for ten years to get them off heroin and into stable housing. Often there are complex mental health issues that require the expertise of a counselor. And sometimes drugs have robbed a person of their cognitive abilities. I would propose, however, that this is the importance of the church. No one person should carry the heavy burden of the excluded on their own. A community, however, can be strong, share the burden, and endure long past the constraints of an individual's energy. In any event, there is perhaps

Abraham

> Bear fruits worthy of repentance. Do not begin to say to yourselves, "We have Abraham as our ancestor"; for I tell you, God is able from these stones to raise up children to Abraham. Even now the axe is lying at the root of the trees; every tree therefore that does not bear good fruit is cut down and thrown into the fire.
>
> Luke 3:8–9 (NRSV)

Luke has gone to great lengths to show us that Jesus' contemporaries were obsessed with who was included in and who was excluded from Abraham's family—the people of God. One common perspective was that one could identify a true child of Abraham from the economic success of a person.[3] Others, like the Pharisees, thought that a meticulous following of Moses's law was the way to be included. Then, as John the Baptist acknowledges above, some would take their inclusion in Abraham's family for granted. But John warns them, the family tree of Abraham is about to be amended. Jesus takes it further, and puts the least likely character, Lazarus, in the place a father reserves for only his young, vulnerable children, his bosom (16:23). And not just anyone's bosom, Abraham's bosom. Indeed, God had raised up a child for Abraham out of the stony ground in front of the rich man's house.

The Kingdom's Challenge

One major mission of Jesus and his Kingdom is to wrap people into God's protective embrace. Just as Abraham will

---

no greater mistake than misjudging the depth of the pit.

3. See Herzog, "Why Peasants," 60.

enwrap his true children after life, so Jesus walked the earth picking up the broken and carrying them through life's stormy weather. How did he pick them up? By listening to their needs, eating dinner with them, healing their wounds, challenging the oft-believed lies, washing their feet, dying for their sins, and crushing the power of death. All he routinely asked in return was trust (faith); a relationship, a commitment to follow. In other words, Jesus worked incredibly hard to include people in God's family and all the person needed do was accept the inclusion.

Is there a Lazarus lying limp at your church's gate? They may wear their wounds on their skin. For others the lazarus-sores are in their mind and heart. My challenge is, let's patiently walk with them by opening our arms and including them in whatever we're doing.[4] Let's do it until our love bursts the veneer of their inner pessimism. Let's do it until they have no doubt that we love them. Let's do it until they believe that God is truly here to help them—ready to wrap them into his fatherly embrace.

---

4. Of course, it isn't always about inviting Lazarus to do what we're doing. It is equally important to join "him" in whatever it is he's doing. Including ourselves in his pit is perhaps the most meaningful move.

19

It Matters Where We Begin

When Jesus came to the place, he looked up and said to him, "Zacchaeus, hurry and come down; for I must stay at your house today." So he hurried down and was happy to welcome him. All who saw it began to grumble and said, "He has gone to be the guest of one who is a sinner."

LUKE 19:5–7(NRSV)

IN HIGH SCHOOL DEREK seemed angry to me. He marked every step of cross country practice with unrestrained and injurious bravado. His well-known accomplishments and outgoing persona made him unavoidable to anyone on our small team. That was unfortunate, I thought at the time, because I would have rather not mingled with him at all. As a freshman I weighed one hundred pounds and only broke five feet in sturdy shoes. On the other hand, I was fast, and you cannot go unnoticed in cross country if you're fast. I beat Derek in the first race of the year, which made me a marked man. For the next nine months I wore whatever downcast name Derek bestowed upon me. Most of the time I just swallowed his anger, but sometimes I pushed back ferociously.

On one occasion, we traveled to the Indiana cross country state championship—as spectators, because we had failed to qualify as participants. We were on the Indiana University cross country course surrounded by several thousand fans and athletes when he came up behind me and pulled my shorts and underwear down to my ankles. Like lightning, I pulled my pants back up and lurched at him with the full force of a five-foot, hundred-pound, embarrassed kid. All I remember is that our teammates pulled me off of him and we didn't speak for a month or more.

I had begun my relationship with Derek living out of my fear of his anger. And so, our relationship developed along the lines of fear and anger. I either avoided him or I fought him. That was our "friendship." My fear prevented me from understanding Derek and the source of his anger. I came into his life at the same time his parents were divorcing. His throbbing temper was all I could see, because my fear made me disinterested in underlying causes. Lucky for Derek, not every Christian in his life began with fear. My hero at the time was a senior named Dave. Dave's easy social skills mixed with profound and committed faith drew me to him. I figured if I could grow to be like Dave that'd be pretty good.

In the spring, Dave carelessly invited Derek to his youth group. I saw this invitation happen and I was shocked at how easy Dave made it seem. I was more shocked that Derek said he'd be there. I knew that Derek thought that all things related to God belonged in a box marked, "for stupid people." Dave broke through that, perhaps because Dave saw through the anger to the pain. Perhaps Dave's invitation pierced the bristly exterior because it spoke so clearly to Derek's hurt. Dave's invitation surpassed Derek's anger because it met so perfectly with his deep need for inclusion.

It Matters Where We Begin

Early the next morning Dave called my house and said, "You won't believe it! Derek accepted Jesus last night!" He was right. I didn't believe it. "Time will tell," I grumbled.

O' me of little faith.

At track practice the next week Derek approached me and talked to me with kindness and respect. To this day, I have never seen anyone change so dramatically so quickly. Derek quickly became one of my closest and most trusted friends. It is to my everlasting shame that my fear kept me from being helpful to Derek before he changed.

I had every reason to grumble about him, you know. He *was* mean to me; no doubt about it. But where we begin with people matters. If we approach people through their sin we are doomed to grumble over them. Jesus begins his relationship with Zacchaeus not with his sin, but with his potential. He begins with optimism for Zacchaeus; an optimism that brims over into a desire to celebrate together. Dave understood the power of optimism. I still struggle with it. I want to make decisions about my relationships based upon evidence, not hope.

Wanting to eat dinner with a jerk like Zacchaeus seems stupid. Fighting him ferociously makes sense. And yet, if Derek had been left to my ferocious care where might he be today? The compassion of Christ has made him a man that has given all his riches away; an educator and coach beloved for his Christ-centered generosity. Beginning with hope changes people. Thank God for Dave; that he didn't begin with distaste for Derek's sin. Dave would have seen Zacchaeus in a tree and said, "Hey! Let's go to dinner!" And I would have grumbled.

20

The Poor Investor

He was made king, however, and returned home. Then he sent for the servants to whom he had given the money, in order to find out what they had gained with it.

The first one came and said, "Sir, your mina has earned ten more."

"Well done, my good servant!" his master replied. "Because you have been trustworthy in a very small matter, take charge of ten cities."

LUKE 19:15–17(NIV)

I WAS IN A car accident in college. That evening a weather system had layered Indianapolis in about a quarter-inch of ice. I drove my friends and I slowly down the highway, but lost control when we came upon a pile up. We slammed into a wrecked car sitting perpendicular to the flow of traffic. We escaped any physical injuries, but not emotional distress. A police officer drove us fifteen minutes to a gas station and left us to find help. For an hour or so, we wandered around the convenience store trying to make sense of the evening's

The Poor Investor

dramatic event. While I paced the candy isle a woman came up to me and said, "My friend and I ran out of gas. Can you help us out?" Now remember, I had just totaled my friend's car, and felt lucky that we were all unscathed. I was not in any place to handle requests with any ounce of wisdom. So I said, "All I've got is this twenty. Will that work?" She snapped the bill out of my hand and said, "Yep." She then waltzed out the door, into her gas-is-empty car, and drove off. Who knows how that twenty was invested. As I realized my foolishness, my stomach sunk deeper into the despair of an already terrible night.

The beginning of this particular parable says that the crowd Jesus is addressing is anticipating him to inaugurate his kingdom as soon as he enters Jerusalem (19:11). Most of them, however, abandoned Jesus at the first sign of violent opposition. In the wake of Good Friday, I imagine some of them felt their stomach sink as they wondered if they'd been cheated. Earlier Peter even vocalized this fear when he said, "Look, we have left our homes and followed you" (18:28b, NRSV). As if to say, *is this venture worth it?* After the cross they must have thought back on this parable and wondered if investing their lives in Jesus was akin to hiding money in a cloth (19:20). Had Jesus, despite all his wonder, turned out to be a ruinous investment? Although, unlike the woman who took my money, Jesus died, taking no one's money with him. So if they felt swindled, it would have been out of their hope and livelihood, not twenty dollars.[1] They were also a people pretty used to disappointment. All this to say, they probably made plans to proceed with their lives, maybe to try and be more cautious the next time a messiah-figure came along. Maybe they pledged to never again be a messiah-enabler.

---

1. In fairness, it isn't as if Jesus was disingenuous. He did warn them, see 18:31–33.

The Upside Down Way

Of course, it wouldn't have taken more than a second look to realize that Jesus himself was making a series of poor investments that would eventually catch up to him. In the past two chapters Jesus has invested in lepers, a tax collector, little children, and a blind beggar. At the same time, he's turned away a very rich and eager man and a handful of respected religious leaders. One wonders if anyone in the crowd surmised that Jesus himself was the fear-stricken servant who put the mina in a piece of cloth. So here Jesus is marching up and into a city occupied by religious zealots and power-brokers and a garrison of soldiers from the world's greatest military force. And what has he invested in to prepare for his "invasion?" What great force has he compiled to thwart the opposition? A brood of prostitutes, tax collectors, little kids, beggars, lepers, and fishermen.

If Jesus managed your retirement account you'd probably pull your hair out.

Of course, the same penchant for dangerous investments that would drive us crazy is what makes him take a risk on us. He invests in us prideful, greedy, bland, broken, addicted, blind, diseased, sexually depraved, emotionally impoverished, and childish people. What's more, he doesn't just invest his grace in us. Or his time. Or his money. No, we're his force for good on the earth.

He's nuts.

Truly, everyday he's laying siege to evil's strongholds *with* broken people. This has two pretty basic pay-offs: first, don't count anyone as a worthless investment, even a woman who swindles us out of a twenty-dollar bill. Second, it is simply not valid to say either, "I'm too messed up to do ministry," or "Now I'm holy enough to do ministry." We do ministry because of his crazy investment in us, not because of our salient minds or ethical prowess.[2] And, I

---

2. Should we then keep on sinning that grace should abound? I

The Poor Investor

think, when we follow him it turns out that he knows what he's doing. Just when we think he's failed, that it was all a big charade, and we've been swindled, he turns one mina into ten, a poor investment into a great one, and death into life.

---

think not. The point isn't that sin should be embraced, but that it has to stop being a blockade to ministry. I know way too many people who for shame, don't engage in ministry. I want them so badly to hear the words of Jesus pierce the darkness of their shame, "Come follow me!" And on the flip side, I know way too many people who wear their ministry as a badge of holiness. I think they equally need to hear that God isn't interested in their badges.

21

All of Patrick

So they asked him, "Teacher, we know that you are right in what you say and teach, and you show deference to no one, but teach the way of God in accordance with truth. Is it lawful for us to pay taxes to the emperor, or not?" But he perceived their craftiness and said to them, "Show me a denarius. Whose head and whose title does it bear?" They said, "The emperor's." He said to them, "Then give to the emperor the things that are the emperor's, and to God the things that are God's."

LUKE 20:21–25 (NRSV)

I LOVE SAINT PATRICK and his story. His holiday, March 17, is my favorite Christian holiday after Christmas and Easter. Much like those holidays, my love for Saint Patrick's Day has nothing to do with the way our culture celebrates. It has everything to do with finding Jesus in Patrick's struggle.

Patrick was a Roman who grew up in Britain. As a teenager his village was raided by Celtic brutes who kidnapped him. They made him a shepherd, isolated him, abused him, and nearly starved him. On a fateful day in the fields he heard God calling him to escape by following the sound of the sea. When he reached the coast there happened to be a boat of merchants about to set off from the harbor. The merchants took him aboard and eventually he returned to his village.

I wonder if these waves of freedom terrified Patrick. For many, liberation can be a terrifying journey. Patrick had to take a gigantic risk to leave his flock for the shore. He knew his captors would feed him eventually, he knew the ins and outs of his blighted life, and he knew staying would at least mean he'd live.[1] He must have suspected that if he went to the shore there was a chance he'd starve to death, or be caught, beaten, perhaps murdered as a punishment. Blissful as they may seem, those waves of liberation are often fraught with risk. Yet, be it faith or courage, or both, Patrick took his chances.

Upon his homecoming, however, he discovered that his village was not the same as he had left it. The Irish marauders had murdered some of his family members. At this point he entered the priesthood and upon completing his education he believed he heard God calling him again, though not to the blissful and liberating sound of waves collapsing on the shore. This time the call was to be a missionary to the very people who had murdered his family and put him through a harsh and merciless adolescence.[2]

This time, the comfort of a priestly education must have tempted him to stay.[3] He probably had a bright future ahead of him as a peaceful abbot or an influential

---

1. It reminds me of the Israelites who wanted to go back to the security of slavery under Pharaoh (Num 14:1–4).

2. For more on the life of Patrick see Cagney, "Patrick," 10–15.

3. Comfortable compared to the life of an enslaved shepherd.

theologian.[4] No guarantee, but I can't imagine either presented the risk of a return to Ireland. At the time, Ireland was the stuff of legend—palaces where heads decomposed on stakes as decoration, tribes often waged brutal and crude war campaigns against one another, and there's even evidence that the Celts practiced human sacrifice.[5] I doubt the monastic life offered such a "romantic" atmosphere. Many an ignorant missionary have journeyed into violent and terrifying scenarios, others, like Patrick, were not ignorant. They were intent. In the way a victim never forgets their abuser's voice, Patrick would have known the landscape of Ireland.[6] Nevertheless, he went and before he died much of the island had seen and accepted Jesus' reconciling love.

What does Patrick have to do with the passage from Luke I quoted above? Well, I think this passage is so often read to mean that God wants us to pay our taxes.[7] In other words, we focus on the emperor bit. I'm not so sure it has that much to do with Caesar. What captures me is, "and give . . . to God the things that are God's." If I take Patrick as my example, it seems nothing escapes God's gaze. What things are his? Well I suppose I get to choose, but I imagine he wants my whole self.[8] I imagine that he wants to draw every bit of

---

4. In the fifth century those were about the most honored careers a man could achieve. An abbot is the overseer of a monastery.

5. For a fascinating book on the subject see Cahill, *How the Irish*.

6. It's worth noting that Christianity existed for a couple centuries in Britain before Patrick. Missionary activity to Ireland, however, was probably scarce. Ireland wasn't a place people wanted to take the Gospel.

7. Which I imagine he does, but I do not think it's the point of this passage.

8. In fact, Jesus has charged the religious leaders with doing just that, choosing to give God a piece of their lives. Part of Jesus' accusation against them has been their straining to give God gifts that people can see, while keeping their hearts untouched by God's

All of Patrick

me toward liberation and every bit of me into a land where I might love my enemies. Whether you need a call to the sound of freedom or to radical servanthood, I hope Patrick's journey will inspire you to give to God what is his.

I'll close with a sample of a medieval Irish poem inspired by Patrick:

> I rise today...
> Christ with me, Christ before me, Christ behind me;
> Christ within me, Christ beneath me, Christ above me;
> Christ to the right of me, Christ to the left of me;
> Christ in my lying, Christ in my sitting, Christ in my rising;
> Christ in the heart of all who think of me,
> Christ in the eye of all who see me,
> Christ in the ear of all who hear me.[9]

---

transforming hands (cf. Luke 11:37–54).

9. "The Breastplate of Saint Patrick," translation from Davies and O'Loughlin, *Celtic Spirituality*, 118–20.

22

Our Last Table

When the hour came, he took his place at the table, and the apostles with him. He said to them, "I have eagerly desired to eat this Passover with you before I suffer; for I tell you, I will not eat it again until it is fulfilled in the kingdom of God."

LUKE 22:14–16 (NRSV)

SEVERAL YEARS AGO I went to a senior art show at a local university. It was a beautiful display of functional ceramics.[1] The centerpiece of the show was a magnificent dinner table, fully equipped with exquisite tableware. The table was aglow with long, elegant candles—as if there was a host expecting to welcome us with a warm embrace and good food. It was quite unlike anything I ever expected to experience at an art exhibit. As it turned out, the artist had indeed used that table and its handcrafted tableware to host a special dinner. A week before the show, she hosted her most

1. When I first heard the term, "functional ceramics," I felt very dumb. Apparently it is the technical term for ceramics that can actually be used (i.e. plates, mugs, cups, etc).

trusted friends, closest mentors, and family for a sumptuous dinner. It was a party to celebrate the culmination of her journey through college, punctuated by the presence of people who had changed her. There was a video of the event on a loop at the show. Much to my surprise, the images of smiles, good food, warm drinks, and laughter made me cry.

I once saw a statue of a man carving himself out of rough-hewn rock entitled, "The Self-made Man." It seems to me that there is no such thing. "Self-made" is an illusion. We can't even eat breakfast without help. Someone planted the oats, cared for the chickens, collected the eggs, raised the pig, boxed the cereal, made the glass, grew and harvested the coffee, shaped the mug, cast the frying pan, and built the house you ate in. Even if you know someone who did all that, someone made the rain fall on the crops, the sun shine on them, the chickens make eggs, etc. Dependence is the norm of human existence. Here in Luke we find a stark reminder that even Jesus chose to not be a self-made, isolated human being. He chose community. He chose to let the disciples into an inner-circle. According to this passage the Last Supper is a celebration of their journey together; an ode to their friendship, their co-laboring toward Jesus' kingdom. The video made me cry, because I know that I would be bereft of shape without my many co-laborers . . . people I'd want at my last table.

What if you had a last supper? Who'd be at the table? There are a lot of folks who wash into my mind when I ask myself that question. There's Stu, a mentor from college who listened to me in a way that empowered my imagination. There's Gwendolyn, who always bumped into me in the university library when life wasn't going my way. There's John, who lived a life of devotion to Christ that made me feel so small, but so full of hope. There's David, who respected me enough to let me into his biggest prayers.

The Upside Down Way

There's Ben, whose faithful humility challenges my every assumption about true greatness. There's Arthur, whose attentive eyes make me feel so valuable. There's Ryan, who makes me laugh like no one else. There's Dan, whose perceptiveness clears a way forward through my overgrown path. There's Sean, who challenges my ever-present notion that I know it all. There's Ed, who walked with me when no one else would. There's Don, whose encouragement seems to ever target my deepest, unspoken fears. There's my wife, who need only say, "I love you," to fill me with long-lost strength. And there are many others, who have and are instruments of God's continuing formation. There are also others who have stalled the work, even squashed my ambitions and desires—people who have often had in common the impulse to speak before listening and to hear but never understand.[2] Most shocking of all, at Jesus' table there's one of those squashers sitting at the table with all the others. If you read John's account of the Last Supper, you'll even notice that Jesus has the audacity to wash the feet of the squasher—John narrates Judas' exit after Jesus returns to the table (John 13:21–30).

The real point I want to get at is what does it take for Christians to co-labor together in a way that puts us at one another's table. Do you need to let people in? Or does the Church need to embrace you? Do you need to get more involved? Does the Church need to bring the involvement to you? Do you feel excluded from the table? Do you know the invitation is open? Is your heart going in a different direction? Is the table already full? If there's a table that is exclusive, I promise you, Jesus is at another table. So how do we create a table of equality? How do we make room for

---

2. Nothing kills a relationship like an unwillingness to listen . . . just consider this country's political landscape. Seriously, listening is, I think, the key to strong relationships in a church.

squashers, like Judas at our table? How do we harness the power of the Last Supper's table? As you can tell, I'm full of questions, not answers. I don't think I'm supposed to admit that in a book.

23

The God Who Suffers and Is with Us

The men who were guarding Jesus began mocking and beating him. They blindfolded him and demanded, "Prophesy! Who hit you?" And they said many other insulting things to him.

LUKE 22:63–65 (NRSV)

EARLY CHRISTIANS FACED A cultural problem. The Greco-Roman world had always believed in the impassibility of God—impassibility means, incapable of suffering.[1] In other words, what happened to Jesus could not have happened to God. For ancient peoples, God was often seen as aloof. The gods of the traditional pantheon had to be manipulated or bribed in order to get them to intervene in human affairs.

---

1. The ancients took for granted that if God were perfect, then perfection would include the absence of struggle or suffering. Another way to think about it is, if something can cause God suffering then perhaps God is not God and the thing that is powerful enough to hurt him is, in fact, God.

The God Who Suffers and Is with Us

Suffering was an inescapable human reality. Conversely, suffering was an unthinkable option for divinity.

Yet here were these Christians claiming that God died; God wept; God sweated blood from overwhelming anxiety; God was flogged; God was punished; God was tried and convicted; God, as it seemed, lost. These were simply inconceivable claims.

So a dilemma confronted these earliest believers in Jesus' divinity. Some developed beautiful ways to explain why God would choose to suffer. Others de-emphasized Jesus' divinity, thereby avoiding the problem. Others still, reimagined Jesus' story and essentially extracted the suffering. One drastic example of Jesus reimagined is called *The Infancy Gospel of Thomas*. It's a story written about a hundred years after Jesus' death and resurrection. It attempts to envision Jesus as a child. Here's an excerpt:

> Somewhat later he was going through the village, and a child ran up and banged into his shoulder. Jesus was aggravated and said to him, "You will go no further on your way." Right away the child fell down and died. Some of those who saw what happened said, "Where was this child born? For everything he says is a deed accomplished!" (4:1)[2]

It reads like a dark interpretation of Superman. On other occasions, this boy-Jesus torments his teacher, kills another boy for messing with a creek that Jesus had parted, lengthens a miss-cut board, and raises a boy from the dead in order to prove that he hadn't killed him. The author of these stories was struggling to communicate Jesus in a method that his culture would understand, but what he did was create a super-Jesus who looked more like the lore surrounding the

2. Pleše and Ehrman, *Apocraphyl*, 13.

The Upside Down Way

Caesars than Christianity's mocked and beaten God.[3] The boy here is not really human, suffering is not an option for him, and he comes off like a divine spoiled brat.

You might read that and be frustrated, but the same thing happens in our world. We don't make Jesus a Greek superhero, but we often allow him to be shaped by our own allegiances and worldviews, rather than the other way around. And, in fact, most of the God-language I grew up hearing had to do with victory and strength. None of my teachers ever tried to reimagine Jesus' character and story like *The Infancy Gospel of Thomas*. Instead, they shaped Jesus with good biblical phrases like, King of Kings or Lord of Lords, minus any mention of his humble commitment to suffering. It was a matter of choosing not to focus on the dark-side of Jesus' story. But the aggregate effect of that focus is that a kid like me still grows up feeling like God is a little bit aloof. I mean think about it. If you feel ashamed, broken, or hurt are you going to go to the superhero Jesus? Only if you have no other choice, for you might catch him in a bad mood.

The disastrous cost of ignoring or undoing Jesus' suffering is that you lose part of the very heart of Christianity.[4] Let me put it this way: we're all going to die. God may intervene for a time to keep us here, but eventually it will catch up to each of us and we will face our own death. And, we will probably face the death of people we really love. Again, God may intervene in those moments too, but for the most part, since death is universal, we will have to

---

3. In fact, it was common for Caesars to have biographers who would write similar fantastic versions of their childhoods.

4. Certainly, it would also be disastrous to focus so singularly on the suffering to forget the victory of the resurrection. Jesus without the resurrection is just a noble martyr. Jesus without his suffering is just a detached God. What we need is to strike a balancing tension between Christ's humanness and divinity.

The God Who Suffers and Is with Us

"watch" people we love suffer. So we *will* suffer.[5] There is no other religion that claims that God knows what that feels like. There is no other God who has faced the pain; no other God who stepped into the universal nature of suffering and took it upon himself. And so, if you can conceptualize Jesus as the suffering God, then you're not alone—only the Jesus who suffers can be near to you in the darkness. If you take the suffering away, on the other hand, you're left with little more than Zeus or some other divine despot.

The destruction of our aloneness was the promise Matthew's Gospel appeals to at Jesus' birth: "'Look, the virgin shall conceive and bear a son, and they shall name him Emmanuel,' which means, 'God is with us'" (Matt 1:23, NRSV). Since we suffer, God can't really be with us without also suffering.

Wherever you are, you are not alone. He has felt the hot sting of a violent fist on his face. He reeled in the emotional torment of betrayal. He has felt the weight of anxiety's desolate cloud. He felt the chill of being alone. He endured the stomach-churning hurt of false accusation. Driven by his loving desire to relate to us, our God suffered.

In the midst of whatever you suffer now or tomorrow, he is not far off. He is not a little superman-brat. He is Emmanuel.

---

5. This is to say nothing of the myriad other sufferings that plague the human experience: depression, mental illness, isolation, betrayal, poverty, hunger, low self-esteem, etc. It's my conviction that Jesus is quite enmeshed with human suffering of every kind.

24

An Upside-Down Sentence

When they came to the place called the Skull, they crucified him there, along with the criminals—one on his right, the other on his left. Jesus said, "Father, forgive them, for they do not know what they are doing." And they divided up his clothes by casting lots.

LUKE 23:33–34 (NIV)

AT THE CENTER OF Luke's crucifixion narrative is one of the most upside-down gestures in all of human story. According to Luke, the ugliest event in Jesus' life was punctuated by clear-headed and unsolicited forgiveness.

Your Bible will likely have a note on verse 34 that reads something like, *this sentence does not appear in the earliest manuscripts.* We do not have the original version of Luke.[1] Scholars assemble bibles using a cache of thousands of manuscripts that span the church's first millennium. This poignant line is only in some of those manuscripts. We will

1. Or any biblical book.

An Upside-Down Sentence

never know why it is in some but not in others. However, we do know that it is a sentiment consistent with Jesus' attitude throughout the book of Luke. It is a lyrical culmination of all of Jesus' upside-down lessons. It's the moment where Jesus puts his money where his mouth is.

Again, I don't know why some manuscripts don't include it, but can you imagine how badly an early Christian might have wanted to edit the phrase out? For the earliest generation of Christians, those who murdered their Lord were not people they would have naturally wanted to forgive. The loss of one's hero or friend tends to incite bitterness and dreams of retaliation. In today's world we often equate forgiveness with passiveness, but no less did the ancients. Retaliation among factions for the sake of honor was a common practice. Families and nations frequently entered into a desperate spiral of revenge. Surely the earliest friends of Jesus felt that pull to hate Rome. Surely some part of them longed for a gospel confined to those not stained with the blood of innocents.

And yet, someone very early on knew this sentence belonged exactly in this place. The church knew that the way of Jesus could not spiral endlessly in exhaustive antagonism between factions. They knew that the good news about Jesus was upside down compared to the narrative offered by any other group. They knew that the cross, and thereby the reconciling blood, was on offer to even the world's merciless butchers. Yes, even the blood encrusted swords of executioners could be beaten into plowshares.

I wonder if this sense of radical forgiveness is somehow slipping away. You must note that none of the soldiers asked for forgiveness. There is no repentance. Jesus acts without any prompting. He, whose hands and feet are pinned to wooden beams, offers uninvited forgiveness. Imagine if such a heart took center stage in our public and private conversations of race in America. Imagine if this upside-down offer dominated our politics. Imagine if it permeated our foreign policy convictions. Imagine if it seeped into your church's view of its neighborhood. Or if it covered your social media news feed.

I think this line is crucial to our understanding of how the Gospel functions. Too often we see the Gospel as something accepted rather than offered; grace as something received rather than given; or the cross as an act of history on our behalf rather than a call to live likewise. When we think of the cross we think of it as a sacrifice for those of us who have accepted, rather than a blood-sealed invitation for the very people we hold in contempt.

Today, take measure of the Gospel you hold dear. Think of it as a manuscript you'll pass down to your children. Does its news look right-side-up or upside down? Have you kept Jesus' plea of forgiveness for his enemies or have you scrubbed it out?

25

Suffering, Even on Sunday

While they were talking about this, Jesus himself stood among them and said to them, "Peace be with you." They were startled and terrified, and thought that they were seeing a ghost. He said to them, "Why are you frightened, and why do doubts arise in your hearts? Look at my hands and my feet; see that it is I myself. Touch me and see; for a ghost does not have flesh and bones as you see that I have." And when he had said this, he showed them his hands and his feet. While in their joy they were disbelieving and still wondering, he said to them, "Have you anything here to eat?" They gave him a piece of broiled fish, and he took it and ate in their presence.

LUKE 24:36-43 (NRSV)

ON FRIDAY THEY STOOD at a distance and contemplated the loss of their hope and friend. How long that Friday must have seemed! They felt the earth quake and their hearts go dark. They saw the sky grow black and their hopes die. They witnessed their friend and teacher give up his last breaths and their faith falter. "Good Friday," is probably not what they would have called it. "Black Friday," or "Disaster Friday," seems more fitting.

Imagine Saturday. It's the Sabbath. They can't go anywhere; they probably didn't prepare food the day before; and if they really observed the Sabbath then they would have done a sort-of-service celebrating and commemorating God's liberation of Israel. Maybe they went to synagogue? These are the last things I would have wanted to do. When it hurts, I tend to want to hide in an isolated shadow. Anything that provokes conversation is on my "list of things to avoid." And maybe that's what some of them did. Maybe they were lapsed Jews for the weekend. Maybe they sat silently together in the very room where they had shared the Last Supper. It is, of course, lost to us. We don't know what they did, but we can infer from Luke's depiction of Sunday that Saturday wasn't so "good" either.[1]

At this point you might expect a pithy, "Christianese" saying, like, "see they had to go through all that suffering so that Sunday could be even sweeter." I actually think this sentiment misses much of the point.[2] As I wrote in chapter 23, suffering is. We suffer. I don't think we suffer so that

---

1. The disciple's reaction to the empty tomb is described this way, "But these words seemed to them an idle tale, and they did not believe them" (Luke 24:11, NRSV). They act out of their despair.

2. I think it is almost always dangerous to try to make philosophical sense out of suffering. But "why" is the question we're always fixated on. So someone says, "Why did my best friend betray me?" A friend replies, "So that God could teach you this lesson." They're both grasping for a reasonable explanation for suffering. The problem with the answer is that it makes God the author of the friend's betrayal. And if God caused your suffering you're likely to feel perplexed and guilty for the grief you feel. I don't think we have to be so roundabout. Why did so-and-so betray you? You'll have to ask so-and-so. But by God's mercy, he shall bring beauty from your ashes. The world is murderous, but God is skilled at resurrection.

Suffering, Even on Sunday

good things will happen. I think we suffer because that is the reality of the broken world in which we live. So Jesus dies, not because he wants to put an emphatic seal on the resurrection, but because his mission was to get us back from the broken world, which is marked by death, so into death he had to go.[3] The resurrection, Sunday, as it were, is the mark of God's mercy—though the world be broken, tears will not go on forever. Suffering, in the finality of Christ's victory, will be eased.

In the meantime, Christ's presence is promised to us in the midst of our suffering.[4] That's why I quoted this particular passage from Luke. Notice this line: "While in their joy they were disbelieving and still wondering . . . ." The disciples are at once joyous and in disbelief. In other words, they're still dealing with the emotional torment of Friday. Sunday is not completely free from suffering. Yet, Jesus does not callously toss them from his presence because of their doubt and emotions. He eats with them. He invites them to bring their struggles to his table. Then he eases their suffering with his presence.[5] That's a huge part

---

3. Hebrews explains this sentiment in several places, but this one struck me as particularly fitting: ". . . but we do see Jesus, who for a little while was made lower than the angels, now crowned with glory and honor because of the suffering of death, so that by the grace of God he might taste death for everyone" (Heb 2:9, NRSV).

4. When the ancient Christian martyr Felicitas was in the throes of childbirth her Roman guard taunted her, saying that if she couldn't handle the suffering of birth, what would she do when she faced the beasts of the coliseum. She is purported to have responded, "Now it is I that suffer what I suffer; but then there will be another in me, who will suffer for me, because I also am about to suffer for him." Perpetua, "Passion of Perpetua," 704.

5. In Luke 24:36–43 the disciples are joyous, terrified, and skeptical. Jesus sticks around with them, settles in with them for a time (Acts 1 says for forty days), and in Luke's final passage it says, "Then he led them out as far as Bethany, and, lifting up his hands,

of the point of Sunday—his presence.[6] I've heard it called, "a personal relationship with Jesus." Yep. He's with you; he's with us. Break bread with him, whether you're living Thursday, Friday, Saturday, or Sunday. Suffering will be until the final Sunday—the eternal undoing of death and suffering. In the meantime, he eases the pain of what we have endured with his gracious and merciful presence.[7]

You have a life to go live. The world, in all its beauty and brokenness, will ever buzz about you. There will be Thursdays of glorious community, dark and bloody Fridays, alone and horrible Saturdays, and even Sundays of ineffable freedom. May we each find that the presence of Jesus' upside-down life gives us what we need to flourish, no matter which day it is.

---

he blessed them, he withdrew from them and was carried up into heaven. And they worshiped him, and returned to Jerusalem with great joy" (24:50–52, NIV). Notice that the terror and skepticism is gone, leaving only joy. He walks with us as long as it takes.

6. Just to clarify, this passage doesn't take place on Resurrection Sunday. I'm using "Sunday," in the metaphorical sense to describe the events after the resurrection and before the ascension.

7. And the church, hopefully, follows the same pattern. We can't undo loss and grief. That's not the goal of benevolence. Instead, we offer our companionship during and through the grief. I think it is really important that we not use overly-simple Christian language to try to undo suffering. We do a much greater service to those who grieve and suffer when we affirm the disastrous nature of their pain, pledge our own tears and our own patient communion, and softly point to the present and coming victory of our Savior.

Bibliography

Cagney, Mary. "Patrick the Saint." *Christian History Magazine* 60 (1998) 10–15.

Cahill, Thomas. *How the Irish Saved Civilization: The Untold Story of Ireland's Heroic Role from the Fall of Rome to the Rise of Medieval Europe.* New York: Anchor, 1996.

Chrysostom, John. *On Living Simply: The Golden Voice of John Chrysostom.* Translated by Robert Van de Weyer. Ligouri, MO: Triumph, 1997.

Davies, James, et al. "The Global Distribution of Household Wealth." Helsinki: UNU-WIDER, 2006. https://www.wider.unu.edu/publication/global-distribution-household-wealth.

Davies, Oliver, and Thomas O'Loughlin. *Celtic Spirituality.* New York: Paulist, 1999.

Foster, Richard. *Freedom of Simplicity: Finding Harmony in a Complex World.* San Francisco: Harper Collins, 2005.

Goldingay, John. *Old Testament Theology: Israel's Gospel,* Vol. 1. Downers Grove, IL: IVP Academic, 2003.

Green, Joel, Scot McKnight, and I. Howard Marshall, eds. *Dictionary of Jesus and the Gospels.* Downers Grove, IL: IVP Academic, 2013.

Herzog II, William R. "Why Peasants Responded to Jesus." In *A People's History of Christianity: Christian Origins,* Vol. 1, edited by Richard A. Horsley, 47–70. Minneapolis: Fortress, 2010.

Kelly, J. N. D. *Golden Mouth: The Story of John Chrysostom—Ascetic, Preacher, Bishop.* Ithaca, NY: Cornell University Press, 1995.

BIBLIOGRAPHY

Malina, Bruce, and Richard L. Rohrbaugh. *Social-Science Commentary on the Synoptic Gospels*. Minneapolis: Fortress, 1992.

King, Jr., Martin Luther. "I have a Dream." Speech delivered at Lincoln Memorial: Washington, DC, August 28, 1963.

Jospehus, Flavius. *Josephus: The Complete Works*. Translated by William Whiston. Nashville, TN: Thomas Nelson, 2003.

Kinnaman, David, and Aly Hawkins. *You Lost Me: Why Young Christians are Leaving Church—and Re-thinking Faith*. Grand Rapids, MI: Baker, 2011.

Perpetua, Vibia. "The Passion of Perpetua and Felicitas." In *The Ante-Nicene Fathers: Tertullian,* Vol. 3, translated by R.E. Wallis, 699–706. Grand Rapids, MI: Eerdmans, 1989.

Pleše, Zlatko, and Bart D. Ehrman. *The Apocryphal Gospels: Texts and Translations*. New York: Oxford University Press, 2011.

Sider, Ron. *Rich Christians in an Age of Hunger: Moving from Affluence to Generosity*. Nashville, TN: Thomas Nelson, 2015.

Thomas, À Kempis. *The Imitation of Christ*. Translated by Aloysius Croft and Harold Bolton. Mineola, NY: Dover, 2003.

Wright, N.T. *The Challenge of Jesus: Rediscovering Who Jesus Was and Is*. Downers Grove, IL: Invervarsity, 2015.

———. *Luke for Everyone*. Louisville, KY: Westminster John Knox, 2004.

www.ingramcontent.com/pod-product-compliance
Lightning Source LLC
Chambersburg PA
CBHW070932160426
43193CB00011B/1661